Student Agency in the Classroom

Honoring Student Voice in the Curriculum

Margaret Vaughn

Foreword by Anne Haas Dyson

TEACHERS COLLEGE PRESS

TEACHERS COLLEGE | COLUMBIA UNIVERSITY
NEW YORK AND LONDON

Published by Teachers College Press,® 1234 Amsterdam Avenue, New York, NY 10027

Copyright © 2021 by Teachers College, Columbia University

Cover design by Pete Donahue

Chapters 1 and 6 contain material from "Making Sense of Student Agency in the Early Grades," by Margaret Vaughn, 2018, *Phi Delta Kappan*, *99*(7), 62–66. Reprinted with permission.

Chapters 1, 2, and 7 contain material from "The Role of Student Agency: Exploring Openings During Literacy Instruction," by Margaret Vaughn, 2014, *Teaching & Learning: The Journal of Natural Inquiry & Reflective Practice*, *28*(1), 4–16. Reprinted with permission.

Library of Congress Cataloging-in-Publication Data is available at loc.gov

ISBN 978-0-8077-6568-5 (paper)
ISBN 978-0-8077-6569-2 (hardcover)
ISBN 978-0-8077-7974-3 (ebook)

Printed on acid-free paper
Manufactured in the United States of America

For my family—Matthew, Mabel, and Marcus
And for all the students who have taught me

Contents

Foreword

With this book, Margaret Vaughn offers a thorough, informative, and altogether inspiring book on child agency. As I read about the importance of child agency to learning, agentic children I have known kept coming into view, speaking to their agency, to their responsive teachers, and to the importance of Vaughn's book.

Vaughn points out that all children have the capacity to be agentic—to be motivated to act on, and have influence within, their worlds. Yet, as Vaughn notes, agency is not simply an individual, decontextualized matter. Many classrooms—acting within district and state requirements—position children as passive receivers of knowledge, not as active makers and users of knowledge to accomplish something important to them. In contrast, Vaughn calls attention to responsive teachers she has known, who, harnessing their own agency, adapt their curricular plans to incorporate the voices, and the visions, of children themselves.

To illustrate and complicate this responsiveness, consider Vaughn's rich story of a 4th-grader named Mae. She had noticed with some alarm the food being wasted in the cafeteria. Mae thought of a recycling plan for the school, and that plan met with approval from her teacher Mrs. Gil. We can imagine how this idea could capture the imagination of many children, not only in her classroom, but in the school. Nonetheless, the plan did not capture the approval of the student council, who, the principal said, had the last word. A barrier arose but, believing in her idea and herself and supported by her teacher, Mae persevered, meeting with individual student council members to sell her idea. Mae was learning the political work entailed in social change.

Importantly, Vaughn notes that Mae's position in the classroom gave her every reason to believe in herself. Her earned "points" as a taker of computerized reading tests, her admission to a gifted program, her inclusion in a teacher-selected group of kindergarten helpers all allowed opportunities for others, and herself, to bear witness to her perceived competence. Yet her classmate James, a designated "troublemaker," did not have such opportunities to reveal his strengths, and Vaughn wonders if he would have had the confidence to put forward an idea and, if he did, how he would be received.

Vaughn thus demonstrates that children are not uniformly supported in pursuing their interests, and, as a result, classrooms and schools lose access to social, cultural, and linguistic resources that children bring to school. She notes that this has the most troubling consequences for minoritized children, since schools have traditionally treated them as just that, "others" with potential learning "problems."

Vaughn's critical words brought to mind a 2nd-grader named Ta'Von from my own experience (Dyson, 2021). Ta'Von had been negotiating a place in the peer world since kindergarten—no easy task for this outgoing Black child in a school serving a majority-White, middle-class neighborhood. In 2nd grade, Ta'Von found the blues; in his journal, he detailed his learning about famous blues guitarists and singers, like Big Mama Thornton and Muddy Waters. Ta'Von could sing the blues too and filled pages recalling lyrics, singing as he did, quietly but consistently. All this knowledge and know-how was ripe for 2nd-grade objectives like learning the features of varied genres (including nonfiction) and opportunities to stretch those objectives (e.g., the blues lyrics drew on his knowledge of Black language). But his teacher had her eye on the language arts textbook assignments and the text-based tests, which had to be turned in to the principal and then the district. Ta'Von found support for his musical motivations and his desires to learn all he could from his church and his grandmother. However, Ta'Von's teacher—and his peers—lost the opportunity to build on his knowledge and know-how.

Professionally smart, potentially agentic teachers abound, and Vaughn offers example from kindergarten to high school of their creative approaches. However, many teachers, like Ta'Von's, feel bound by constraints. We hear how middle school environmental science teacher Tammi and high school social studies teacher Les both had interactive classrooms that encouraged students to develop their sense of agency to rethink history, take action to solve current problems, and work toward a better future. However, both teachers were also compelled to abandon their teaching visions and prepare their students for their mandated reading and math tests.

Vaughn's book is particularly important in these neoliberal times. Education has become a commodity, its quality measured by standardized test scores and its means too often driven by mandated textbook-driven curricula.

Throughout, Vaughn draws on her rich experiences as a teacher and a researcher to explain and illustrate vividly for us the multiple dimensions of agency. She demonstrates with classroom vignettes from primary to secondary the many unique approaches teachers take to develop and support agency in their students and thereby improve their academic and socio-emotional learning. It will take all educators—teachers, principals, district administrators, and state and federal policymakers—to create the educational contexts our children deserve.

—Anne Haas Dyson

REFERENCE

Dyson, A. H. (2021). *Writing the schoolhouse blues: Literacy, equity, and belonging in a child's early schooling.* Teachers College Press.

Acknowledgments

Writing a book like this is a collection of my years and experiences as a student, teacher, researcher, university professor, and parent. I feel honored to be able to write this book on behalf of so many inspiring students and teachers. This book would not have been possible were it not for them. A special thank you for the generosity of the students and teachers who shared their experiences, thinking, and ideas with me. Thank you to my many friends in the work who have talked with me over the years about agency, ideas, and everything teaching and learning related. Your thoughts and friendship have propelled me forward. Finally, thank you to my family, Matthew, Mabel, and Marcus, who are my everything, and continue to remind me daily of how what we think and do matters. And to my readers: thank you.

Introduction

The initial inspiration for this book came from an experience I had in my very 1st year of teaching. It was the first few weeks of school and a shy, 6-year-old student, named Jackson, wrote in his journal, "Bush hog." Having lived in cities my whole life, I had no idea what a bush hog was, but I excitedly asked, "What does it eat?" and "Tell me more about it." Jackson would shrug or say something too soft for me to hear, until finally, after several days, he exclaimed, "Bush hogs don't eat anything. They're farming equipment!" We both laughed, and I explained that I didn't know much about farming. Then something fascinating happened—something that I, as a new teacher, had never seen before: All of a sudden, Jackson became a leader. Since I obviously had a lot to learn about farms, he decided he would come up with important agricultural topics for us to discuss. From then on, whenever he had time to write and draw, he would create a new chapter book about farm life and read it aloud to the class.

I didn't know what to call this shift in Jackson's attitude from compliant and reserved to fully engaged and excited to direct his own learning until several years later when I began studying for my doctorate. What my student had developed, according to researchers, was *agency*, which, broadly speaking, refers to students' desire, ability, and power to determine their own course of action (whether that means choosing a learning goal, a topic to study, an activity to pursue, or a means of pursuing it).

Scholars have studied agency in and out of schools. Dorothy Holland et al.'s (2001) work on identity and agency and Anne Haas Dyson's (1986, 1997, 2003, 2020) work about children's ideas and power provide a powerful voice in the discussion of student agency in schools. The compelling ideas presented in Holland et al.'s work (2001) about how agency allows for powerful interactions to occur in one's life offers a convincing rationale as to why agency is part of the fabric of who we are as individuals. Dyson's (1986) pivotal work on children's roles in relation to their agency and how classroom events are reshaped by children to afford opportunities for agency provides a productive lens to understand that student agency is in fact observable and codeveloped in classrooms with teachers *and* students. As Dyson (1984) articulated, agency is cultivated as children "interpret a task and (make decisions about what should be done when) in greatly differing ways" (p. 235). Thus, student agency is a meaningful lens that can be used to understand how to create learning contexts in schools where students are in charge of their own learning.

As a practicing classroom teacher, agency seemed essential in teaching. Within my research of my practice as an elementary school teacher (Vaughn & Faircloth, 2013), I noted that my students often veered away from the assigned instructional tasks and reshaped learning tasks to engage in activities relevant to their interests and lives.

In fact, my students demonstrated sophisticated ways of enacting agency, such as constructing plays with peers during a classroom activity meant to be performed individually, making posters instead of practicing math skills, and interviewing their friends about books they made during a silent reading activity. As I began to explore the research on student agency to examine this important-yet-elusive aspect of classroom instruction, what I found was that there seemed to be a wide gap between theories of agency and classroom practice. For example, consider an example from a situation in which there are clear opportunities to support student agency, but these valuable opportunities are overlooked. Fourth-grade students in Ms. Buckner's class listen to the directions of how to complete a worksheet on the concept of main idea. Students are asked to read a passage about the use of exercise balls instead of chairs in a school district across the country. After the directions are read, Madie raises her hand and asks the teacher and her peers, "Can we do this? Can we write about this to our principal?" Ms. Buckner redirects the class back to the objective of completing the worksheet. Madie raises her hand again and says, "But Ms. Buckner I know a good fundraiser—we can ask the principal about getting bouncy balls to sit on. If we did this, and we get enough money, I think we could get this for our class and the other 4th-grade classes." Once again, Ms. Buckner redirects the class to get back to completing their worksheets.

This experience reflects those moments during classroom instruction where teachers have the opportunity to build on student inquiries and promote student agency (Vaughn, 2014). Johnston (2004) outlines the dialogue teachers can use to build on students' agentive narratives like this. Students like Madie are integral to enhancing rich learning experiences by offering their suggestions and directions during classroom interactions. During these moments, teachers like Ms. Buckner have the opportunity to build on their students' ideas and co-create learning outcomes with students so as to support students' agency and ownership of their own learning.

Although Ms. Buckner could have seized this opportunity to develop Madie's idea and her agency in this instructional situation, she redirected her students to get back to the assigned worksheet. Unfortunately, such opportunities to capitalize on student agency are often missed or dismissed by teachers in many classrooms. But why? Perhaps one reason Ms. Buckner was unable to capitalize on the opportunity to promote student agency is that agency is not something we discuss in a concrete manner in teacher preparation coursework or during professional development. Another possible reason is that Ms. Buckner, like many other educators across the nation, is working within the constraints of high-stakes assessments and mandated curricula efforts, which confine teachers' abilities to adapt the curriculum to better meet their students' needs (Hoffman & Duffy, 2016; Ravitch, 2010; Vaughn, 2019). In today's educational climate, unfortunately teachers are too often positioned without professional agency themselves:

> Teacher professional discourses are to a large extent as they are because of the teachers' positioning within their professional environments, and their agency (or lack of) is heavily influenced by factors which are often beyond their immediate control. (Biesta et al., 2015, p. 629)

In fact, since educational reform efforts like the No Child Left Behind Act of 2001 (NCLB), there have been continued efforts to standardize the curricula, which continue to restrict teachers in their efforts to adapt and build on students' inquiries and interests during classroom instruction (Botzakis et al., 2014). Au (2007) described how teaching and accountability reform efforts are deeply flawed because they restrict teachers' capacity to focus on nontested subjects and emphasize a teacher-centered approach rather than a student-centered approach to learning.

Madda et al. (2011) echo such a claim and emphasize that, all too often, educators today are pressured to promote instruction that centers on unrealistic tasks related to "doing school rather than doing life" (p. 44). As a result, student agency is virtually nonexistent across the curriculum, as opportunities to cultivate student agency are missed and tasks are often taught that are "unauthentic, unrealistic, and by implication, not useful for engaging in real-world activities" (Pearson et al., 2007, p. 36).

However, agency is more important than ever as a deliberate dimension of classroom practice that actualizes a view of learning that supports students' identities, backgrounds, culture, linguistic capabilities, and interests. Specifically, in the context of schooling, student agency is "a student's ability to have ideas, intentions, and to exert influence and take actions in the learning context" (Vaughn, 2018, p. 6), and to have these initiatives honored. When students are able to act on their sense of agency, they are more likely to engage in learning, take the initiative to be in charge of their learning, develop dispositions as active learners that extend beyond simply learning tasks, and position themselves as active rather than passive learners (Brown, 2020; Gutstein, 2007; Johnston, 2004; Vaughn, 2020).

AN ORIENTATION TOWARD THE NATURE OF LEARNING

Valuing student agency or not during instruction is based on a key assumption about the nature of learning. In a theory of learning that values most highly the transmission of knowledge, the teacher directs the learning context by transmitting knowledge to the student (Doyle, 1983; Winne & Marx, 1982). Accordingly, within this view of teaching through a transmission lens, an emphasis on a teacher-centered and a skill-and-drill approach promotes passivity (Alvermann, 2001). However, when learning is viewed as a complex site where students engage in the learning, question the world at hand, and make meaning of the learning situation as a way to inform their world, school, and learning, student agency becomes a critical aspect of classroom instruction. Agency is socially mediated and constructed. It is "the strategic making and remaking of ourselves, identities, activities, relationships, cultural tools and resources, and histories, as embedded within relations of power" (Lewis et al., 2007, p. 18).

THE SOCIAL CONTEXT

To understand agency within complex social contexts like the classroom, individuals position themselves and are positioned during learning events. Agency is a "social event that does not take place in a void or in an empty wilderness" (van Lier, 2008, p. 163). This social view of agency emphasizes the ways in which individuals respond and interact in complex social environments, such as the classroom, in relation to their agency. For example, in a classroom, students can act (1) independently or with peers, (2) as a whole class, and (3) in response or opposition to the social dynamics of the particular situation. As such, within this frame of agency and a complex view of learning, teachers are instrumental in structuring classroom opportunities and building on the potential for student agency. For example, Sharma (2008) found that when teachers provide spaces within the curriculum for their students, "rich possibilities for meaningful learning" occur (p. 297). By structuring the curriculum to include meaningful tasks, authentic to students' lives and interests, students become increasingly interested and vested in learning (Cavagnetto et al., 2020; Hatt & Urrieta, 2020). As a result, students may be more likely to develop agency where they question, challenge, and ultimately negotiate their position within what Dyson (2020) terms an "all too tight curriculum" (p. 119).

A cornerstone of agency is the ways in which learning is viewed and how curriculum is shaped and structured. Purcell-Gates et al. (2007) highlight how learning tasks and activities can impact and influence the ways in which students participate within the curriculum. Similarly, Ghiso (2011) found 1st-graders took the lead in the direction of their learning by participating in authentic tasks that they considered important and relevant to their lives. Students wrote complex narratives relating their family experiences to important historical figures in the civil rights movement. In doing so, students, harnessed a sense of agency as they actively participated and set the direction of the lesson. This teacher recognized that even in 1st grade, students bring their worlds to the classroom:

> Students were able to set their own agendas for their work—naming a topic that merited exploration in writing, deciding what to share and with whom, devising plans for writing, and interrogating their work's importance . . . the class centered on situating writing within a culture of questioning and further investigation. (Ghiso, 2011, p. 354)

Like this civil rights project, one possible way to promote student agency is for educators to structure classroom tasks that are meaningful and anchored in students' interests and inquiries. This view of learning emphasizes how instruction can be anchored in authentic tasks, relevant to students' lives. Such a view can disrupt the skills-based approach that is currently emphasized in many school districts across the country. Gambrell et al. (2011) suggest that meaningful tasks extend beyond teacher-directed tasks and are designed to focus on "communicating ideas for shared understanding rather than simply to complete assignments or answer teacher-posed questions" (p. 22). Relevant tasks include opportunities for students to learn for a real purpose through tasks based on students' histories and their own lives and are embedded in culturally relevant pedagogy (Certo et al., 2010; Dyson, 2003; Gay, 2002; Genishi & Dyson, 2015; Souto-Manning, 2010).

Instruction that focuses on culturally relevant practices and authentic and engaging tasks are essential. When students are empowered to act on their sense of agency, they take action and initiate the direction of the instructional situation. By opening the curriculum to students' linguistic and cultural backgrounds, as well as their interests and inquiries, a collaborative space can be constructed whereby students can help to provide direction in the curriculum and learning outcomes (Schipper et al., 2020; Tobin & Llena, 2010). In a study of Mexican-descent students, Reyes (2009) found that when teachers invited students' lived experiences into the curriculum, they "support[ed] their academic endeavors and provide[d] a renewed sense of agency for them to continue on their trajectory toward being and becoming successful students in school" (p. 112).

As teachers recognize and build on student inquiries, spaces to foster student agency are created within the curriculum. For example, Mitra (2004) found that high school students were able to "articulate opinions to others, construct new identities as change agents, and develop a greater sense of leadership" (p. 662) when invited into school decisionmaking. In short, when teachers and schools recognize *and* embed students' interests, cultures, backgrounds, linguistic strengths, and identities into the fabric of classroom learning opportunities, opportunities for student agency are forged.

Such a view of learning supports a sociocultural perspective of agency where learners are situated in complex and dynamic learning contexts. Student agency is interdependent and mediated by teachers, other learners, and the individual's actions and intentions during learning situations, as well as the situational variables that work to support agency. Within this socially mediated view of agency, individuals are collectively and individually shaped by their participation and nonparticipation during classroom practices. Bloome et al. (2004) highlight this multilayered and dynamic socially constructed view of agency in the ways in which individuals "act on the situations[,] . . . build on what has occurred in the event[,] and collaboratively create the event and the series of meanings that constitute the event" (p. 7). In this way, student agency is multifaceted and functions as a jointly constructed action between teachers, students, and peers. For example, the teacher structures specific activities with students during learning experiences, where students are active participants, acting on and within the instructional situation to co-construct their agency.

Agentic learners are human beings enacting their full potential to change their world (Freire, 1970). As a result, students are active co-constructors within particular learning experiences; they interact, participate, and negotiate the meaning of these activities. Giddens (1979) reinforces this view of agency as the ability to reinterpret or to reinvent one's thinking. Theoretically, within this view, student agency can be found in the ways in which students develop their own stance, taking charge of their learning by responding, questioning, and exerting influence in the learning context to transform the learning context. Supporting student agency is needed now more than ever in today's highly politicized educational system—our students need it and so do our teachers. This book is meant to engage in critical reflection about the nature of agency in today's schools and to facilitate discussions about student agency in classrooms today, helping teachers promote it in their students and teaching them to recognize and value their own learning initiatives.

OVERVIEW OF THIS BOOK

The book is divided into two parts. Part I, Locating Student Agency, consisting of Chapters 1–4, describes what agency is in classrooms and how agency matters more now than ever in schools in the nation and can become a core remedy as we seek to find new ways to better support the learning of students historically marginalized in our broader culture and in our schools. In this section, I also show how theoretical perspectives informed a model of agency based on relevant literature and research that I conducted in elementary schools over the last 10 years. Here and throughout the book, readers will find mini case stories rich with ideas that they can adopt in their own teaching and classrooms. (All names of students and teachers are pseudonyms.)

In Chapter 1, a definition of agency is provided based on relevant research in schools and theoretical perspectives. A model of agency is conceptualized, outlining three core dimensions needed to cultivate agency: dispositional, motivational, and positional. A discussion of why student agency matters more now than ever in classrooms is provided.

Chapter 2 further explores the dispositional dimensions needed for student agency: purpose and intentionality. Using research and theoretical understandings of agency aligned within these dimensions, discussion focuses on these integral components.

Chapter 3 addresses how motivational dimensions of agency are instrumental in a model of student agency. These theoretical orientations include understanding how persistence and perception inform how structures and supports can develop student agency.

Chapter 4 provides a discussion of the positional dimensions of a model of agency. The role of interaction and negotiation are central components needed to support student agency in classrooms. This final component within a model of agency is central when thinking about ways to construct opportunities for student agency.

Part II, Growing Student Agency, consisting of Chapters 5–9, focuses on specific measures educators and schools can take to cultivate agency in the classroom. Through research, classroom vignettes, teacher interviews, and conversations with students, I show what agency looks like on the ground in today's schools from a variety of perspectives, across disciplines and all grade levels. Teaching for agency can be a challenging process, one where we must acknowledge the challenges teachers face daily in their work to balance a variety of constraints. I share examples and conversations with teachers and students about the nature of agency. Teachers show great creativity in not only responding to student initiatives but creating opportunities, like the teacher who invented a weekly "sound off" in which students regularly wrote about something that was important to them, read their essays, and led class discussions of their topics, often leading to collaborative projects for addressing a problem or issue.

In Chapter 5, discussion focuses on what agency means to students. Understandings are developed through interviews with students to provide a portrait of what agency means according to the ones who experience it and need it the most.

Chapter 6 provides a discussion of what teachers say about agency and its role during instruction. Interviews from teachers are shared, as well as descriptions of classroom practices used to support structures for student agency.

Chapter 7 provides examples of how to teach for student agency. Taking the theoretical model of agency described in Chapters 1–4 combined with student and teacher feedback in Chapters 5 and 6, this chapter provides core strategies about ways to teach for student agency in classrooms.

Chapter 8 is the culminating chapter in the book and outlines strategies on how to create a culture of agency in the classroom and schoolwide. Practices that support student agency are detailed.

In Chapter 9, the final chapter in the book, I conclude with a focus on the future. I pose the question, "What could happen in schools if we offered rich spaces for student agency?" Discussion centers on how student agency is a central tool in reshaping the narrative in schools today that often emphasizes a student deficit perspective. A collaborative way of thinking about how teachers, teacher educators, and school leaders can promote and cultivate agency is discussed.

This book is designed to provide educators at every level, and across all disciplines, with the underlying research and theoretical rationale for this key educational force, along with an understanding of the distinguishing dimensions of student agency, the practical means to incorporate it into instruction and curriculum, and a wealth of examples that will model ways to either start slowly by putting a toe in, or to jump into the deep end in order to cultivate student agency as a liberating means to empower all learners in today's highly charged educational landscape.

Part I

LOCATING STUDENT AGENCY

CHAPTER 1

What Is Student Agency?

The development of agency is often described as a critically important goal for all students. Countless school mission statements speak of the need to help young people become independent thinkers. Colleges and universities expect high school graduates to be self-driven learners. And business leaders call on K–12 education to prepare the next generation of problem-solvers and entrepreneurs. Today's students must develop agency, or the "capacity—the ability to think unconventionally, question the herd, imagine new scenarios and produce astonishing work" (Wan & Gut, 2011, p. 10). A central aspect of student agency is the ability for students to act on and modify their world and to develop an entrepreneurial stance (Bilac, 2012). As students enact agency, they "give significance to the world in purposeful ways with the aim of creating, impacting, and/or transforming themselves, and/or the conditions of their lives" (Basu et al., 2009, p. 345). However, two obstacles have impeded a common understanding and implementation of student agency in the field of education.

First, test-based school accountability as promoted by the No Child Left Behind Act (2002) and U.S. Department of Education (2009) created pressure on teachers to provide highly directive instruction, offering few opportunities for students to make choices about what and how they learn. For example, consider the plight of Kayla, a teacher with whom I work. Kayla, who teaches third grade in a school with an 88% Native American student population, found that the state's prescribed literacy curriculum lacked attention to Indigenous culture, so she adapted instructional resources and materials to give students options to study oral storytelling, visit and learn from community elders, and read culturally responsive texts. However, because the school was designated as not meeting adequate yearly progress (AYP), Kayla's supervisors were desperate to raise test scores, and they reprimanded her for straying from the state's pacing guide and text selections, which they believed were more closely aligned to state tests.

Or consider Tammi, a middle school science teacher, who teaches in a school with a high population of English language learners (ELLs). In our research together, Tammi emphasized that her role in the classroom was a facilitator. She expressed that her desire was to foster and create critical thinkers and students who would realize and seize their potential. She described how she viewed her role as facilitator and that developing a classroom climate supportive of individuality and creative freedom was essential.

Tammi explained that using prepacked science units was not culturally relevant and was distant from the type of instruction she knew would support her students' inquiries. She described the importance of developing instructional units based on her students' interests and questions and the need to examine the local environment as a site for exploration and critical inquiry. For example, during one exchange she shared, "I want to create critical thinkers. I want to teach them how to seek the knowledge on their own, how to question it. I want them to know that I don't have all the answers and that they need to find answers on their own" (Vaughn, 2013, p. 126).

To work toward this, Tammi developed several units where she asked students to examine local environmental problems. In one lesson, she asked students to document the extent to which pollution eroded a school marble structure, right outside of the school's front doors. She emphasized that teaching about local issues in an authentic manner was essential to develop critical thinkers. She reasoned that her teaching had to be relevant and engaging so that students could make connections with devastating environmental impacts in their everyday lives.

Structuring opportunities like this was an essential dimension of Tammi's approach to teaching. She provided opportunities for students to present their ideas, interrogate their findings, and ask more questions about what they learned. Other lessons were just as engaging. For example, Tammi developed a mock trial lesson where students debated the impact of environmental hazards in their everyday lives. She emphasized that these types of lessons encouraged critical thinking and helped her students see the impact of their choices in the real world. Tammi reasoned that providing her students with an opportunity to share their voice and engage in the decisionmaking process was an essential characteristic of what she knew was effective and authentic teaching.

Although Tammi taught environmental science, a subject not yet assessed by the state, she described the challenges her school and colleagues faced with the approaching assessments. In fact, Tammi's school was in what she termed "AYP jail," a term she used to describe how her school was restricted by the constraints of AYP because it hadn't seen student achievement growth in 2 years (Vaughn, 2013, p. 127). What resulted was a testing preparation blitz where teachers across the school, like Tammi, were asked to participate in school-wide test preparation. This meant that for a month leading up to state assessments, Tammi had to stop teaching environmental science and prepare her students on test-taking strategies and practice worksheets for the state tests in mathematics and reading.

And finally, consider Les, a secondary social studies teacher, who emphasized that he wanted his students to adopt a critical view of history and develop a social awareness about local topics and issues. He developed units of study focused on national issues of equity and the rights of immigrants. He shared that he wanted students to think and find answers for themselves. However, as the school year approached standardized testing, Les was also faced with the pressures of standardized testing and schoolwide policies that forced him to engage in testing blitz preparations. He reasoned that providing students with opportunities to question and adopt a critical stance about history and current events was in stark contrast to the school's goals of raising test scores. Ultimately, Les was unable to reconcile teaching in an authentic manner with the realities of standardized policies and procedures he believed were too distant from what his students needed to become critical thinkers who held social awareness about history and current events. At the end of the school year, Les left his position as a classroom teacher and returned to the private sector.

According to many personal accounts and research studies of educators' behavior over the last 15 years, Kayla, Tammi, and Les's stories are not unusual. When teachers make it a priority to strengthen their students' sense of agency, say by encouraging them to choose topics, texts, and activities that meet their linguistic, cultural, and instructional needs as well as activities rooted in students' interests, their decisions can easily be vetoed by supervisors who insist that they follow a prescribed curriculum or conform to "skill and drill" practices (Berliner, 2011; Howard & Miller, 2018; Onosko, 2011; Vaughn, 2020). However, 21st-century learning skills emphasize the need to develop skilled students who have the propensity to develop an entrepreneurial stance and imagine alternative possibilities, leaving little room for prescriptive approaches to teaching and learning (Moses et al., 2020).

Even if educators agree in principle that students should become agentic and independent, they may struggle to translate that goal to classroom practice, or they might find themselves at a loss for words, unsure how to talk about such issues. Several months ago, for example, I asked a group of teachers to tell me their thoughts on student agency. I happen to know that some of these teachers routinely encourage their students to pursue self-directed research projects, contribute to decisions about class rules and structures, and voice their opinions in class discussions. However, when I posed my question, they gave me a blank stare and asked, "What's student agency?"

But the bigger problem is that the precise definition of student agency remains elusive, even among scholars who study it. While it is easy to give a broad definition of agency in general—it refers to students' ability to define and act on their own goals—it can be hard to pin down the details. For example, is agency a psychological concept, having to do with an individual student's motivation, confidence, and self-determination (Deci & Ryan, 1985; Reeve & Shin, 2020; Ryan & Deci, 2017)? Does it have more to do with personal and social development, such as the effort to shape an identity for oneself in school (Ferguson et al., 2015; York & Kirshner, 2015)? Is it better to think of it in political terms, having to do with students' power to challenge teachers' biases or unfair school practices (Abodeeb-Gentile & Zawilinski, 2013; Toshalis, 2015)? Does it have to do with organizational structures, such as rules about how students are supposed to dress and behave in school (Jackson, 2003)? Or, at a deeper level, does agency have to do with how people use language, such as the ways in which teachers control classroom discussions, allow students to talk freely, or encourage them to speak with authority (Cook-Sather, 2020; Johnston, 2004)?

While researchers talk about student agency in a dizzying assortment of ways, the various approaches can be grouped into three main categories: dispositional, motivational, and positional (see Figure 1.1). These three dimensions of agency can be used to conceptualize a framework of student agency, which, taken together, conceptualize a holistic framework of agency.

The first dimension includes research that focuses on students' personal dispositions, such as the extent to which they possess purpose and intentions. This dispositional dimension can be related to how students are entrepreneurial, hopeful, generative, creative (Garud et al., 2007; Oakeshott & Fuller, 1989; Tran & Vu, 2017), self-directed, and determined (Snyder et al., 1991). On this dimension, developing

Figure 1.1. Broad Dimensions of Agency

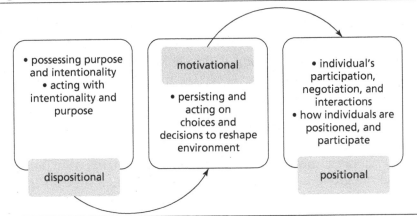

a sense of agency has to do with having *purpose* and *intentionality* and the ability to take action in response to opportunities. This includes research that focuses on students' inner dispositions and how individuals use knowledge of themselves, understandings based on past accomplishments, and ideas for future goals (Archer, 2000; Bandura, 2001).

On the motivational dimension aspect of student agency, students' perception and their beliefs about whether they can persist to complete desired actions inform this layer of agency. In this way, students' ability to make plans, regulate their own emotions and behaviors, and reflect on their own skills, as well as the extent to which they value what they are doing (Bandura, 1986; Ryan & Deci, 2000) underlies how motivation intersects with student agency. This includes research that examines the role of *perception* as well as *persistence* to continue despite perceived obstacles or barriers (Garcia et al., 2015).

The third dimension, positionality, includes research into the ways people participate, negotiate, and interact in groups, communities, and organizations. Here, agency has to do with understanding one's social, cultural, and historical environment; the *interactions* and *negotiations* (Wenger, 1998; Vygotsky, 1978); the identities formed in practice; and the ways in which students are positioned in complex learning environments.

Although it may appear that agency is the same as other related constructs (e.g., motivation, engagement, self-efficacy), agency is multidimensional and not solely about one's motivation or self-efficacy or about an individual's disposition. Agency weaves together properties across these dispositional, motivational, and positional dimensions and works to understand how students negotiate these dimensions within complex social contexts such as the classroom. In fact, we may miss one or more of the dimensions if only looking at one component. For example, Christian and Bloome (2004) in their study of independent reading and writing groups found that a group of predominantly male ELL students had strong beliefs of themselves as writers and their ability to create stories. However, when working within the group, a more dominant, female, White reader was given control of the pen by the teacher because the teacher believed her ELL students were not able to lead the group in the activity. As a result, the ELL students in this classroom were positioned outside of the activity. Like in this example, race, sex, and smartness (Hatt, 2012) are critical elements that are integral in discussions about student agency. Teachers and schools are instrumental in suppotring or detracting student agency.

Without careful reflection and the ability to notice how all three dimensions (i.e., dispositional, motivational, and positional) work together, teachers and schools may potentially miss opportunities to support student agency. In other words, agency is not solely about one's disposition, motivation, or how they are positioned. Student agency is interconnected along all of these dimensions and underlies how students interact within complex social environments where tools and resources can allow for or shut down opportunities for agency.

In spaces where teachers are aware of how these dimensions inform their practice, students are able to take the initiative to be in charge of their own learning and engage in learning to expand opportunities. Examples of students using their agency include students offering their opinions about lesson topics, generating ideas, and having and using their intentions to design, problem-solve, and inform classroom activities and projects in their communities. When classrooms allow for student agency, learning experiences move beyond a transactional approach of learning to one that is co-constructed and generative.

School opportunities indicative of agency can be found when students make choices, act on their intentions, and take actions in their efforts to develop their own positions and opinions. In these environments teachers are adaptive and flexible in their approach to teaching. They do not teach to their students but with and alongside them as they integrate their knowledge of effective instruction with students' individual learning needs, interests, and ideas.

Figure 1.2. Inner Dimensions of Agency

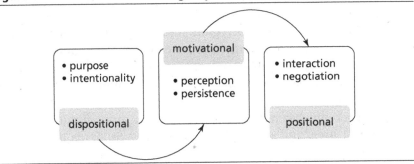

To promote student agency, then, teachers should address all three of these dimensions. They must support (or at least try not to get in the way of) students' efforts to define themselves as independent learners. They must ask students to reflect on what they've learned, what has been hard for them, what has gone well, and why. And they must create a classroom environment, norms, and rules that allow students to make meaningful decisions about what they want to learn and how they want to participate in the group. These three dimensions can be broken down even further, encompassing theory and research that exemplify a multidimensional view of agency.

As Figure 1.2 indicates, student agency is comprised of these interrelated dimensions: purpose, intentionality, perception, persistence, interaction, and negotiation. (More detail about each dimension can be found in Chapters 2, 3, and 4.)

These interrelated dimensions of agency are defined as follows:

- *Purpose* references how students have a vision or ideas related to their goals and ideas.
- *Intentionality* underlies the ways in which students possess the willingness to pursue their ideas and intentions.
- *Perception* is the ways in which students see value in what they are doing.
- *Persistence* is the ability to persist in the face of obstacles and barriers.
- *Interaction* references how students exist in a complex environment with competing social demands and variables.
- *Negotiation* is the ways in which students negotiate and balance their beliefs and desires and enact their identities in practice in complex social communities.

These dimensions can be seen at work in the following classroom scenario. In a 4th-grade classroom in the Pacific Northwest, after a series of local forest fires in the region, a fourth grader asked questions during a science unit on energy. She posed questions about where the forest fires originated, how they began, and why, if the fires occurred in California, the class could smell the smoke in another state (Idaho). Excitedly, teachers and students wrote these questions on chart paper and together embarked on a journey to learn more about wind patterns, forest fires, and geographical landmarks. Students interviewed one another, eliciting even more questions about fires in the region, and developed a plan to pursue their inquiries (Vaughn, Premo et al., 2020).

The teacher structured special research time each day for students to work on this project. Experiences like this signify student agency and the interplay between teachers and students as they co-construct learning opportunities together. This student's belief in her vision and the way in which she valued what she was doing were central to her pursuing and developing her ideas. In this exchange, students and teacher pursued their ideas and transformed the learning activity to make it more relevant to their inquiries. In doing so, students developed the identity in practice of someone capable of transforming and influencing the learning context. As a result, students harnessed agency as they exerted influence to open new opportunities to learning.

The student was instrumental in harnessing agency in this situation, but so were her teacher and peers. Teachers can structure specific practices to engage and support students in developing their ideas. In this example, the teacher could have easily redirected the student instead of supporting and encouraging her to pursue her ideas. Options for building and co-constructing learning opportunities that facilitate student agency occur all the time during classroom instruction. Think back to Madie in the Introduction who presented a class activity proposing replacing student chairs with bouncy balls. Although Madie's teacher did not seize the opportunity to build on her agency, the opportunity presented itself. Teachers must be willing to notice these opportunities and structure learning supports and ultimately flexible contexts that are conducive to expanding on students' agentic opportunities.

This is not to suggest that it's always simple to notice and redirect one's instruction to support opportunities for student agency. In fact, there are serious tensions involved in providing opportunities for students to harness their agency. Consider Kayla, Tammi, and Les.

For these teachers, redirecting their instruction to support students' interests and ideas was a constant struggle that put them at odds with their administration. Many teachers face conflicts in justifying activities where their students have agency.

For example, given federal, state, and local directives, many teachers are strongly encouraged to use scripted literacy programs to ensure student success on state assessments.

Despite renewed emphasis on the Every Student Succeeds Act (ESSA) (U.S. Department of Education, 2015), which suggests a broader lens on school success, including measuring school climate, educators continue to be restricted in their efforts to justify developing opportunities for student agency. Discussions about student agency are needed now more than ever between teachers and administrators as they work toward reshaping learning activities that look beyond standardized outcomes to create a more equitable space in schools.

A model of student agency that weaves together psychological and social dimensions (i.e., purpose, intentionality, perception, persistence, interaction, and negotiation) connects how three core dimensions of agency—disposition, motivation, and position—can be conceptualized to understand agency in learning contexts. In the following chapters, these dimensions are further discussed using relevant literature and classroom vignettes.

EXTENSION

Cultivating student agency requires careful reflection and the ability to critically examine how the three dimensions (dispositional, motivational, and positional) work together.

1. Reflect on your own schooling experiences. What were some opportunities where you felt you had a sense of agency as a student? Why did you feel this way? What did you value in the experience? What materials and resources were made available? How did teachers and school-wide personnel support/detract your efforts?
2. Have conversations with a couple of students about how they feel about their agency in school. Ask students the following questions:
   » Can you share a time when you were able to take an idea and pursue it in class?

» Were there any obstacles? If so/if not what did you do? Did others help?
» What did this experience show you about yourself as a learner?

You can also consider the following conversation with Quin, an 8th-grader, about his experiences. As you read it, ask yourself these questions:

- How did this experience support Quin's sense of agency?
- What could have been potential obstacles Quin/the teacher experienced?
- What strategies could have been employed to overcome these obstacles?

THE CASE OF QUIN

Quin says this about school: "[It] is boring for the most part. We don't really have time for doing what we want because we have to switch classes a lot and only have like 50 minutes with our teacher." One area where Quin expressed he had more autonomy was in his science class: "I'm into skateboarding—everybody sees me skate. I told my science teacher I wanted to do stuff on skateboarding." At first, he thought she'd say no, but instead he shared, "We started talking about it. She asked me what about some of problems I have when I skate—like when I'm at the bowl [outdoor skate park] and I want to get faster but can't with the area that's there." Over several weeks, Quin researched the outdoor skate park, the curved surfaces needed to help skaters gain more speed, and the cost and materials needed to expand the outdoor park. With the encouragement of his teacher and school, Quin presented his findings to the city's parks and recreation department for consideration.

CHAPTER 2

Purpose and Intentionality

Think about it, if you were a kid, wouldn't you want to be able to make decisions about what you get to do in your class?

—5th-grader, male

Agency is largely voluntary and based on how individuals use knowledge of themselves, understandings based on past accomplishments, and ideas for future goals (Archer, 2000; Bandura, 2006). In this way, agency relies, in part, on students' inner dispositions. Thus, understanding how agency is constructed along this inner, dispositional dimension provides a necessary link toward understanding how students become active agents in schools that are complex, social institutions. Inden (1990) captures his relationship:

> Agency is the realized capacity of people to act upon their world and not only to know about or give personal or intersubjective significance to it. That capacity is the power of people to act purposively and reflectively, in more or less complex interrelationships with one another, to reiterate and remake the world in which they live, in circumstances where they may consider different courses of action possible and desirable, though not necessarily from the same point of view. (p. 23)

Agency relies on individuals possessing a purpose and giving significance to the world in which they inhabit and remake. Think back to Jackson in the Introduction and his experience with bush hogs and agricultural topics and the essential role of purpose and intentionality in his agentic pursuits. Jackson had a clear purpose for sharing his ideas and thoughts about his life experiences with agricultural topics. He wanted to teach others about his knowledge and life out of school. Without this sense of purpose and intentionality, which manifested in a series of complex actions such as producing chapter books and leading class discussions, his actions would have possibly fallen short.

Purpose and intentionality, two primary theoretical constructs, outline how individuals' dispositions are central to student agency. The role of purpose and intentionality are essential precursors to one enacting agency; without purpose and intentionality, one is left without a focus and may be unable to negotiate and act on their ideas. In the following sections, these two inner dimensions are outlined to conceptualize the dispositional dimension of agency.

PURPOSE

Purpose reflects a persistent and generalized objective to accomplish something that is at once meaningful to the self and leads to productive engagement within the world (Bronk, 2013; Damon, 2008; Damon et al., 2003). Purpose has the following distinct elements:

- Goal directedness: The ability to possess a goal or objective and pursue what is needed to meet that goal
- Commitment: A promise to complete one's goal
- Personal meaningfulness: The extent to which an individual finds meaning and purpose (Bronk, 2011)

These dimensions can be seen in the following classroom scenario. After reading the book *Crenshaw* by Katharine Applegate, a story about a family experiencing hardships and homelessness, Marcus, one of the students in Ms. Mehan's class, sparked interest in developing a school-wide foodbank project. In Ms. Mehan's class, students were frequently encouraged to share their ideas, work collaboratively to accomplish their goals, and seek guidance from Ms. Mehan as needed to pursue their interests. Typically, in this class, Ms. Mehan encouraged students to collaborate to develop their ideas.

To begin the foodbank project, Marcus and his classmates developed a plan to accomplish their goal. They created signs (see Figure 2.1), wrote about the foodbank for the class newsletter, and shared their ideas with other classrooms in the school. Ms. Mehan was instrumental in this process, as were Marcus and his classmates. Ms. Mehan opened an instructional space in her classroom where students were encouraged to pursue their interests and ideas. Over the next several weeks, Marcus and his classmates could be found outside of the school as parents were dropping off their children, sharing the information about the foodbank (Vaughn, 2020).

Figure 2.1. Food Drive Sign

Marcus and his classmates held a purpose for their work, which resulted in a sense of personal meaningfulness. Students created targeted goals of starting a food drive, thereby committing to the task of creating a food donation site at the school and sharing the news via newsletter and morning announcements with the school. In this way, their purpose served as a compass, guiding and navigating students' path toward completion (Mariano et al., 2011). Students demonstrated their commitment as they worked steadily on these goals over the next month. Goal directedness and personal meaningfulness were evident as students met their targeted goals and continued with the project. In this way, Marcus and his classmates aligned their actions to fulfill their purpose.

Purpose is an organizing principle, providing young people with a coherent vision of their future that connects in meaningful ways to their

present life. So, for example, purpose can infuse young people's oth-
erwise seemingly mundane everyday activities, like schoolwork, with
a heightened sense of motivation, relevance, and direction (Koshy &
Mariano, 2011, p. 13).

Purpose is associated with indicators of academic success in students as well as socioemotional learning goals and nonacademic measures. For example, in young adults, Hill et al. (2016) found that having
a sense of purpose supported feelings of being able to attain future
goals. Bronk (2013) found that when youth possess a sense of purpose
in their life, that can lead to high self-esteem and psychological well-
being. Further, Hill et al. (2016) emphasize that "there is increasing
evidence that individuals may begin to commit to a purpose during the
adolescent and emerging adult years, and that doing so can serve as a
catalyst for success in meaningfulness in life" (p. 258). Such evidence
suggests the importance of supporting and developing a purpose in students, not only as central in creating classroom learning environments
conducive to agency but as an important dimension of lifelong success.
    One tangible way to model the importance of possessing a pur-
pose is to incorporate purpose-building activities in the classroom and
school (Pizzolato et al., 2012). For example, teachers can notice, listen,
and embed learning activities driven by students' intentions and their
visions, much like Marcus and Jackson (Introduction). Opportunities
to build on students' intentions and facilitate discussions about purpose can model to students that they can act with their agency to suc-
cessfully exert influence and take actions.
    However, despite compelling support for fostering a sense of pur-
pose in students, interestingly many schools seem to fall short in doing
so. Hill et al. (2016), in their review of studies that examine teaching
for purpose, found that while schools have a unique and powerful
opportunity to develop purpose in students, few schools actually do.
Similarly, Mariano et al. (2011), in their examination of how a group
of Black middle school adolescent girls conceptualized their sense of
purpose about the important things in their lives and goals and intentions for their future, found that schools weren't as influential in supporting their goal; rather these adolescents were most influenced and
supported by mentors and supports outside of school. Schools should
work with and alongside of communities to invite mentors to help
cultivate youth's sense of purpose.
    Without supporting a sense of purpose in students in the class-
room, opportunities for agency and meaningful participation in

schools are missed. Think back to Madie in Chapter 1 and her idea for hosting a fundraiser to purchase bouncy balls for students to sit on in the 4th-grade classes at her school. Rather than supporting and developing her vision for this project, the teacher redirected the class back to completing the worksheet. An important opportunity was lost in the process. Schoolwide and classroom structures and supports must be in place to capitalize on students' visions and creative pursuits. Schools are there to support students, but oftentimes students are seen as powerless people (Scherff, 2005). Steps toward reshaping such a view included understanding and embedding a sense of purpose and intentionality in the work we ask of students.

A central aspect of purpose is commitment and intentionality. In fact, purpose and intentionality are deeply connected. Once the path has been set, (i.e., purpose) students need to pursue and act on their ideas and intentions. Much like students with whom we interact, we too must harness purpose and intentionality in the work that we do. For example, when I was thinking about writing this book, several driving questions came to my mind: What is my purpose for writing this book? How can I do this? and What supports do I need to accomplish this task? Students ask these same questions when they exercise their agency every day in classrooms. What am I doing? Can I do this? Do I want to do this, and if so, why? What will occur as a result of my actions? In other words, central in their agentic pursuits is the underlying inner drive of whether students possess purpose or intentionality in the task at hand.

Take for example, one of my 1st-grade students, Nicole, who was determined to learn how to read. She was not content to read the short, familiar texts so many of her classmates read. One afternoon, instead of heading to recess, she went to the school library and checked out a lengthy children's version of the story of King Lancelot and the Knights of the Roundtable. She held a deep purpose of wanting to be able to read books of her own choosing, and her intentions guided her despite being faced with several challenges to complete that text (which she eventually did after voluntarily sitting in at recess, every day for 2 weeks, working on reading that text). She held a firm purpose for accomplishing this task and a sense of commitment toward reaching her goals.

In this manner, understanding the role of purpose and intentionality in relation to constructing agency is useful when conceptualizing how students develop this inner dimension of agency. Purpose underscores how students possess a vision, an idea, as well as an understanding and a willingness toward intentions, ideas, activities, and learning events. Intentionality supports how students think and believe they can achieve their goals and the extent to which they possess not only a commitment but willingness to act on their ideas and determine their own course of actions. In the following, this inner dimension is further explored.

INTENTIONALITY

In the research literature, intentionality has evolved as a concept rooted in psychological domains since the 1980s when the term became related to one's ability to regulate and to determine one's course of action (Deci & Ryan, 1985). Intentionality implies an understanding of one's self and ideas and a willingness to act on one's ideas. In the context of schooling, intentionality can be viewed as a student's willingness to have their own ideas in learning events. For example, consider a recent exchange I had with a group of students during an after-school book club. Before our book club time, I encourage students to reflect on the day and share any ideas that may have come up for them. During an exchange, students were excited about starting a book drive after hearing that some of their peers didn't have books at home. They started discussing next steps and listed several obstacles they may come across (e.g., how to find books, how to deliver books without other children feeling spotlighted). If students are unwilling to grapple with ideas and pursue their ideas, even if others disagree, they are unlikely to be able to branch out during learning to follow ideas that align with their individual needs (Vaughn, Premo et al., 2020).

Intentionality relies on the extent to which students can act as entrepreneurial, generative, creative (Tran & Vu, 2018), goal-directed, determined (Bandura, 2001), or resistant meaning-makers (Reyes, 2009). Oakeshott and Fuller (1989) suggest that intentionality is paramount in conceptualizing agency as "one recognize[s] as having an understanding of [them]self in terms of [their] wants and [their] powers and creates opportunities" (p. 35). Those who act with agency have intentions and take the initiative to act with an ability to create opportunities to expand their world.

Most scholars who study intentionality contend that self-determination is a cornerstone of how individuals decide and pursue their intentions. Scholars further suggest that it is this role of the individual in determining their own course of action based on intentions, beliefs, and ideas that capture how individuals pursue and achieve their goals. Self-determination is the "exercise of self-influence in the service of selected goals and desired outcomes" (Bandura, 2006, p. 165). As such, a central tenet of self-determination theory underlies how individuals have a sense of self, or self-realization, characterized as "knowledge of themselves and their strengths and limitations to act in such a manner as to capitalize on this knowledge" (Wehmeyer et al, 1996, p. 22). For example, students in the context of a learning activity make decisions about whether to pursue a specific learning task based on measuring if they are able to do it, if they want to do it, and if the task benefits what it is that they want. Self-determination focuses on an individual's tendencies to make choices and decisions in the context of their actions.

Within the broad framework of self-determination theory, basic psychological needs theory (BPNT) (Deci & Ryan, 2000; Ryan & Deci, 2000, 2017) has been proposed as a mini-theory aimed to underlie the role of social and emotional support of individuals in their efforts to act according to their intentions. BPNT posits that three psychological needs (i.e., relatedness, competence, and autonomy) outline a theory of self-determination. According to Ryan and Deci (2017), relatedness is defined as the need to be connected and accepted by significant others in a specific context; competence reflects the need to effectively interact with the environment and to experience a sense of accomplishment or achievement; and autonomy refers to an individual need to experience freedom and choice in action. For example, Evans and Liu (2019), in their research of high school music students, found that students who had a higher sense of relatedness were more likely to undertake solitary practice, to develop competence and autonomy. These students recognized that undertaking solitary practice would potentially increase their ability to engage more fully and skillfully in their role as musicians.

Consider the following synergy between self-determination and intentionality. In classrooms where teachers support students' intentionality, learning looks vastly different than a teacher-directed approach to learning. When students can choose tasks of interest and work with peers of their choosing and materials of their choice, they gravitate toward learning that is relevant and meaningful. Learning in this manner is "nondidactic; is embedded in meaningful activity; builds on the learner's initiative, interest, or choice (rather than resulting from external demands or requirements); and does not involve assessment external to the activity" (Rogoff et al., 2016, p. 358). In learning contexts supportive of students' intentions, teachers are facilitators and provide the necessary supports for students to take control of their own learning.

In a recent observation of a 5th-grade coding class, these tenets of self-determination are palpable. During a coding lesson, students must make several decisions based on their ideas. During one observation, I interviewed a 5th-grade student about her coding process:

Sonya: Today we are using our bots to circle around the trash can.
Me: Why are you doing that?
Sonya: I get to decide what I wanted my bot to do today—what path, what code, and how far it has to go.
Me: Tell me, how do you do it?
Sonya: Well, first you have to think about what you want to do, like in this line here; do you want it to go this way or that way? Each line affects it [the bot] and how it'll go.

(Sonya's teacher, Ms. Wessner, walks around and sits next to students, asking them about their plans and ideas for their bot.)

In this conversation with Sonya, I realized that Sonya believed she was able to do this. She had choice in all aspects of this activity—from deciding what she was going to do with her bot to deciding what line in the code to add and how and where her bot would go. Sonya was in a community of other coders within a classroom setting where she was given the necessary support she needed when she needed it. Ms. Wessner sat alongside her students, asking them questions at their own pace and specific to what they needed depending on the particular idea they presented. Sonya felt competent. Although it is hard to capture her level of competence in the exchange, her excitement, enthusiasm, and confidence were evident while watching her input a line on her computer and then as the bot moved the intended way.

Her teacher, Ms. Wessner structured the class so that students had a deep level of autonomy, from deciding on what and where their bot went on that day to encouraging students to try multiple ways and paths. Her language encouraged her students to want to try regardless of the outcome. Johnston (2004) emphasizes how self-determination is aligned with dialogic exchanges like this between teachers and students as he shared, "[A]s teachers, then, we try to maximize children's feelings of agency…[and] the belief that the environment can be affected . . . [and] that one has what it takes to affect it" (p. 39).

Maximizing and encouraging students' intentions for the work they create and do is essential when cultivating their agency. Undergirding this is the belief that students' three psychological needs are met (relatedness, competences, and autonomy; Deci & Ryan, 2017). In other words, when students have these needs met, they are more likely to engage in learning; take the initiative to be in charge of their learning; develop dispositions as active learners, which extends beyond simply learning tasks; and position themselves as active rather than passive learners. Feeling a sense of autonomy leads to internalized views of what is needed to maintain this (Ryan & Deci, 2017), thereby supporting student agency.

Purpose and intentionality work in unison. Intentionality is at the core of what drives students to take a chance on their purpose and their ideas. It is a student's willingness to believe in their purpose that enables them to take actions needed to pursue their intentions. Students are active agents in the complex world of school. Their inner dispositions are an integral part of the making of their own agency. Students must not only have a willingness to act but must be purposeful in their actions. Thus, developing a sense of agency has to do with having *purpose* and *intentions*.

Agency is interdependent—developed through purpose and intentions, but also mediated by teachers, other learners, and the resources and materials available in learning contexts. In this way, agency is co-constructed between individuals, collectively produced, and negotiated in practice (Holland et al., 2001). Viewing the classroom as a complex site emphasizes how students use tools and resources to fulfill their intentions and purposes. Holland et al. (2001) emphasize how students negotiate and co-construct their identities as individuals with purpose and intentionality through improvisations (a process of "making worlds"). Bakhtin (1981) uses the term *self-authoring* to refer to this process in which identities and agency are continually co-constructed. Through this process, students negotiate their sense of who they are and what they believe they are capable of doing. Student identity, skill, and agency are therefore codeveloped as they interpret and improvise within such settings.

USE OF TOOLS: SELF-DIRECTED SYMBOLIZATION AND IMPROVISATION

Through self-directed symbolization and improvisation (Holland & Lave, 2009), students negotiate their purpose and intentions and initiate actions toward these goals. Self-directed symbolization, according to Holland and Lave (2009), is where, within a specific situation or encounter, a student's collective life experiences take up the cultural resources at hand to produce a self-guided response to that encounter.

Think back to Jackson who used his collective life experiences to create and provide chapter books to the class about his knowledge about agricultural topics.

Through self-directed symbolization and improvisation, Jackson was able to pursue his work and creations about his collective life experiences of living on a farm. Like Jackson, students hold intentionality and purpose and use cultural, linguistic, and background knowledge to imagine possibilities and opportunities based on their intentions, ideas, and purpose. Self-directed symbolization and improvisation are necessary tools in the process of students directing their agency.

Through improvisation, which manifested in creating chapter books, leading class discussions, and writings on agricultural topics, Jackson harnessed agency. Improvisation and self-directed symbolization are necessary tools when thinking about how students use intentionality and purpose to pursue their ideas and beliefs. Oftentimes this results in innovative activities (e.g., Jackson creating chapter books); visual representations (Figure 2.2); and dialogue as students pursue their intentions and purposes.

Figure 2.2. Wishtree Poster

Schools cannot necessarily provide students with intentionality and purpose; however, "they can provide opportunities for purposeful engagement and elucidate the connection between present and future work to help students think more intentionally about future goals" (Summers & Falco, 2020, p. 49).

Consider Mabel: After reading the book *Wishtree*, about an immigrant girl who experienced violence in the community but was brought together by the community's wishtree, a tree where community members posted wishes, by Katherine Applegate, Mabel was inspired to start a wishtree at her school (Vaughn, Premo et al., 2020). To begin the process, she created a poster describing her idea and purpose for the wishtree at the school. Supporting students' ideas like this, however, requires sharing the instructional floor with students, where teachers invite students' backgrounds, interests, and inquiries into the classroom while balancing the demands of teaching in oftentimes highly restrictive contexts.

Because students are situated in learning environments, where they are positioned as the learners, there can be a tension between teachers viewing the learning process as one where knowledge is transmitted to students versus a view of students as knowledgeable meaning-makers. In order to fully cultivate student agency, teachers and schools must accept that students come to school with rich cultures, languages, and out-of-school experiences. Teachers and schools must be willing to value and listen to students' purpose and intentions. It requires flexibility in that teachers must not only acknowledge the unpredictability of the classroom environment but also invite it in to cultivate a dialogic classroom; one where students and teachers are in dialogue together. In doing so, rather than adhering tightly to prescriptive curricula, teachers are flexible and invite their students into the curriculum. Students' histories, beliefs, understandings, and ideas are central to the learning environment (Vaughn, 2016). Sawyer (2004) explained the importance of creating these open, inviting spaces in classrooms and the essential role teachers have in structuring such spaces: "[T]he teacher creates a dialogue with the students, giving them freedom to creatively construct their own knowledge, while providing the elements of structure that effectively scaffold that co-constructive process" (p. 14).

We can see these types of learning spaces in a variety of disciplines and across the literature. Zhang et al. (2019) examined the structures and supports needed to support youth participation in science, technology, engineering, and mathematics (STEM) coursework in middle school. The teachers structured STEM learning opportunities in a flexible curriculum, termed "Invention Education," which focuses on providing students with opportunities to invent, pursue their ideas, and create inventions based on real-world problems and ideas of interest to students.

Teaching invention requires that students lead the direction of the learning situation. It is a shift from traditional teaching methods to one where students and teachers enter conversations about what it is they are learning together. Zhang et al. (2019) found that middle school students were highly engaged and learned advanced science content based on their participation and interactions during the unit. The lead teacher in the project emphasized the shift needed to teach in a way that afforded students the flexibility and creativity to pursue their ideas: "Teaching invention requires a shift from traditional teaching methods focused primarily on the transmission of knowledge to more open-ended facilitation that encourages students to actively acquire and apply science knowledge to invention activities" (Zhang et al., 2019, p. 247).

Similarly, during an integrated arts and social studies lesson, Johnson (2019) found that high school students developed confidence and a sense of agency as they were supported to pursue historical events or significant figures through a variety of modes: poetry and the arts. By opening the curriculum to afford students to engage with the arts and to pursue topics of interest, students actively engaged in the learning process as they used primary sources and poetry to create multimodal representations of what they learned.

In a unit on computer game authoring, Johnson (2017) found that middle school students learned knowledge of programming and higher-level mathematical concepts while planning game interactions and specifying events and actions. Significant to this research in relation to student agency is that teachers structured explicit lessons focused on programming language but then scaffolded students as needed in their creations. In other words, the teachers structured a gradual release of responsibility (Pearson & Gallagher, 1983) where the teacher structured explicit support and then gradually reduced the support as needed. Webb et al. (2019) emphasize that this dynamic is "a balance between the extremes of teacher responsibilities and student responsibilities" (p. 76). As a result, students were encouraged to self-select peers to problem-solve and create their games with guided support as needed.

In younger children, Dyson (1986, 1997, 2020), in her account of detailed stories about students' out-of-school lives, suggests how the classroom space allows for improvisation and self-directed symboliza-tion, guiding students in their work as readers and writers.

> Indeed, any kind of symbol making is motivated by an intention grounded in the relations and interactions—the practices—of daily life. Vygotsky points to play as the site for the dawning of symbolic activity. A box, for example, is just a box; but, depending on its size, a box could be trans-formed by children's talk and action into a home for hiding out, eating, and sleeping; or, as one steers and all make travel plans, it could become a car for going down the road; or maybe, if the box is small, it could become a baby for rocking . . . or maybe just an item for sale in a pretend store. (Dyson, 2020, pp. 120–121)

Much like in these classroom examples, classroom structures are not fixed but must shift in a variety of ways to support students' pur-pose and intentions and ultimately their agency. Teachers who sup-port student agency are flexible within these learning environments. Without these flexible learning environments, where students are en-couraged to use a variety of resources to produce self-guided responses to situations and improvise, opportunities for students to harness their agency are stifled.

Students are agentic individuals who develop their agency in sociocultural contexts and in relation to others (Clarke et al., 2016). Imperative to supporting agency is understanding purpose and intentionality and how these dimensions inform the develop-ment of student agency. Students use self-directed symbolization and improvisation to pursue their purpose and intentions. Teachers are instrumental in cultivating learning spaces and opportunities where students are encouraged to pursue their intentions and purpose and use self-directed symbolization and improvisation in their agentive pursuits. In the next chapter, perception and per-sistence is described to understand the motivational dimension of agency.

EXTENSION

1. Consider your experiences with developing purpose and intentionality in your schooling life experiences and/or adult life. What supports were in place, what obstacles derailed you? Why? What did you need to be successful in your efforts?

2. Pull out a few of the student cases described in this chapter (e.g., Marcus, Nicole, Sonya, Mabel) and identify what the student's purpose was for their respective project. Reflect on the following questions:
   » What steps did these students need to take to pursue their ideas? Was there a clear purpose?
   » What materials and resources were necessary for students to pursue their ideas?
   » What could have been potential obstacles in these experiences, and how might these have been overcome?

CHAPTER 3

Perception and Persistence

If a teacher gives me busy work and it's usually worth nothing, I still have to do it no matter how I feel. If I want to learn a certain way, most of the time I can't do it my way, I have to do it the way the teacher says.

—11th-grader, female

Students are situated in contexts that can support or detract their ability to harness their agency. Understanding how students possess the willingness to wrestle with their ideas and intentions, possess the belief that they can accomplish the goals they set forward, and take courses of action to accomplish what they set forward in the face of perceived obstacles is crucial. Thus, perception and persistence are central along the motivational dimension of a model of student agency.

PERCEPTION

Students are more driven to learn when they set their own paths for what it is they want to learn. Their perceptions of the activities they are asked to do, and their ability to reshape activities to make them more relevant to their interests, informs how the role of perception is instrumental in the development of student agency. Archer's (2003) notion of reflexivity, or the "courses of action [that] are produced through the reflexive deliberations of agents who subjectively determine their practical projects in relation to their objective circumstances" (p. 135), is a productive lens to view how students take courses of action in complex learning communities in their learning pursuits.

For example, consider Mae, a 4th-grade student who wanted to start a lunch recycling program at her school. She searched online and found how other schools developed a recycling program. She created a fact sheet to share with her teacher and principal that included the amount of projected waste in her school. She shared her fact sheet and plan with her teacher and principal.

When students share their ideas and questions in schools, opportunities for cultivating their agency are easily transparent. However, rather than taking up her idea and supporting her efforts, the school principal shared that such a project had never been done and that in order to make changes, Mae would need to take her ideas to the student council—a fair request that further worked to try and instill collective student agency in the school. However, the student council shut Mae's idea down, and the principal sat back and offered little discussion about the topic. Despite this, Mae met for monthly scheduled meetings with student council members and talked about the importance of recycling in the cafeteria. She shared her findings of just how much waste milk cartons produced for 1 week at the school (Vaughn, 2020). During this experience, Mae possessed the belief in her ability to continue with the project, she held value and interest in what she was doing, and she persisted when faced with a choice to abandon her idea or to continue despite the student council's opposition. In doing so, Mae weighed her courses of action against these perceived constraints.

> Czerniewicz et al. (2009) emphasize that "students' experience[s] of constraining factors are mediated by their own constellations of concerns and what students actually do occur as a result of individual reflexive processes in which their concerns are considered in relation to the objective reality of structural enablers and constraints." (p. 84)

In other words, Mae was heavily interested and vested in pursuing the lunch recycling program. As a result, she perceived that the activity had value and was one she was willing to pursue despite the obstacles she experienced. In this way, the role of persistence and perception were central in her pursuits as she engaged in reflexive processes to measure whether she wanted to pursue the lunch recycling program. In schools, learning projects like this can be further conceptualized into activities or tasks.

A central factor in how students make decisions and choices as to whether they are willing to pursue and persist is in their view of the tasks. For example, students ask the following questions: Is this task interesting? What about this is relevant to my life and learning? When can I use what I am learning by doing this? In this way, students' ability to persist with a task aligns with their perception of what it is they are doing and the extent to which they value it (Wigfield & Cambria, 2010). Similarly, students shut down and avoid doing what they perceive as too challenging or impossible. It's similar to the old tale of Goldilocks: If something is too hard, it won't work; if it's too easy, it won't work either. It has to have the just right balance in order for students to continue with a task.

Accordingly, task valuing has been found to be a dominating factor in how students develop motivation across a range of subjects and contexts (Ball et al., 2016; Merga & Roni, 2018) and how they can demonstrate their agency. That is, when students value what they are doing, they believe they are capable of doing the task at hand and they continue working on the task to engage in the necessary effort needed to perform it. As a result, in order to create agentic learning opportunities in schools, tasks must be structured in such a way where students are interested in and value what it is that they are doing and find that it is meaningful and relevant. Thus, tasks must possess the following characteristics:

- Interest value, how much the individual likes or is interested in the activity
- Attainment value, the importance of the activity
- Utility value, the usefulness of an activity (Wigfield & Eccles, 2000).

In addition to interest, attainment, and utility value, students must believe they can perform the task and make decisions to pursue and persist with a task to its completion.

PERSISTENCE

Persistence is the ability for individuals to steadily maintain effort and engage in an action or complete a task (Yen et al., 2004). A variety of psychological dimensions, including self-efficacy (Bandura, 1977, 1993) and task choice (Dweck, 2012; Pintrich & Garcia, 1993, 2012), defined next, are instrumental when understanding how individuals persist in contexts to enact their agency.

- Self-efficacy, or the belief of one's ability to perform the task well and the extent to which they value the task greatly informs whether a student has the desire to engage in and pursue their ideas and interests (Ainley, 2006; Bandura, 2001).

- Task choice outlines how individuals choose and make decisions to pursue their interests, ideas, and intentions (Pintrich & Garcia, 2012).

Developing agency has to do with each of these interconnected concepts (self-efficacy and task choice). That is, in the context of schooling, a student has to have interest in doing the task, believe they can perform the task, and make decisions to pursue the task to its completion. In this manner, students then make decisions to persist in their learning pursuits. If there are barriers, students make decisions, much like Mae, to persist or abandon their pursuits. Agency has to do with how tasks are structured, who is afforded opportunities, and how individuals make these reflexive decisions as they weigh what it is they want to do within complex social environments. Social interactions, classroom structures, learning opportunities, and the activities students take up help to recursively shape how these variables manifest.

However, agency is not solely dependent on an individual simply deciding to persist, and through their interactions they achieve agency. Social contexts are key when considering how students enact their agency. Supportive contexts and structures in schools are central in fostering opportunities for students to continue to pursue their ideas and interests. Students exist in complex social environments where they interact and work alongside peers, and their teacher, agency, and ability to take actions to support their ideas and intentions do not solely reside within. For agency to work in a classroom, teachers and schools must be willing to construct opportunities with and alongside their students.

For instance, in the previous example, Mae could have been met with a teacher or principal who vetoed her idea. If this occurred, Mae would have had to make the decision to continue with her idea and find other ways to make her project continue. However, perhaps in that situation, because Mae was positioned in such a way where she was discouraged, she may have been more likely to abandon the idea (i.e., given that the principal said no). Positionality, discussed in Chapter 4, is an essential dimension of student agency that cannot be undervalued.

However, a lack of persistence is often discussed solely in terms of psychological terms, such as being intrinsically motivated (i.e., Mae possessed the inner desire to want to create the lunch recycling program at all costs) without attention to how students are positioned.

Careful attention and critical reflection must occur in understanding students' positionality within the learning environment, instructional interactions and structures, and the broader social and cultural experiences that affect how students enact their agency in schools.

In fact, based on popular views, one might be tempted to suggest that Mae needed to persist and possess grit in her pursuits in this scenario where she was told no. Simply possessing grit emphasizes that to succeed one needs "to fall down seven times and rise eight" (Duckworth, 2017, p. 45). However, conceptualizing and equating agency as a matter of persisting doesn't take into account the learning environment and the broader historical, political, and racial inequities that have kept many children behind in the history of schooling.

Historically, students have been discouraged and/or denied agency in schools, particularly students of color, students who are living in poverty, and students from homes where English is not the primary language (Cramer et al., 2018; Ferrada et al., 2020; Flores & Rosa, 2015). The structural inequality in schools seldom leads to contexts where students can merely persist, or for that matter succeed by simply acting with grit. Students are positioned in schools that can afford or detract their efforts to pursue their ideas and interests.

Agency is multidimensional and relational, connecting students, teachers, their peers, and the broader system of schooling. Students are positioned in ways that can afford or detract their ability to pursue their purpose and passions. For example, consider one of my good friends, Leila, a first-generation, multilingual, Latinx college student. She is successful by many accounts: She has run several successful businesses, has a thriving family, lives in a nice house, and so on. On all accounts, she is an accomplished individual. However, through the lens of persisting and grit in schools, she failed. Well, really schools failed her, but let's think about her learning trajectory.

Leila went to a private, predominantly White, upper-class school in the Northeast for high school after being awarded a scholarship given her placement exam scores. Then, she was awarded a scholarship to attend an Ivy League school for college. However, after 2 years, she dropped out of college. It wasn't an issue of Leila simply persisting or possessing the grit needed to graduate and succeed (if we viewed it solely on this lens, her success after college would indicate that she indeed had grit and persistence). Instead, institutions failed her: the needed guidance and support in high school about being a student of color in a predominantly White upper-class high school, the lack of necessary structures and systems to support her during her transition into college, and ultimately the necessary supports to fuel her ideas and interests.

It can be reductionist to solely look at an individual and view their ability to be successful and possess agency as merely "simply getting up." It just doesn't afford a realistic portrait of how students interact in complex social environments and doesn't address issues of race, sex, and class and the many realities and inequities of schooling and society. Unfortunately, stories like Leila's are the norm; there are countless experiences and examples of bright individuals who lacked the supports, structures, and systems in schools to support and fuel their ideas and cultivate their agency in the context of schooling.

> A focus on grit is taking a heavily impoverished view of human motivation; in the long run, most people do not persevere at things because they are good at persevering, they persevere because they find things that are worth investing in. The implication for school is that they should spend less time trying to boost students' grit, and more time trying to think about how their offerings could help students develop purpose and passion. (Mehta, 2015, p. 331)

Developing agency is by no means solely dependent on the shoulders of students—hence the idea that students must simply have grit, persistence, or agency, for that matter, doesn't take into account the sociopolitical influences embedded in schools that position and allow access to some and not others. The communities of practice lens (Wenger, 1998) allows for an understanding of how individuals achieve and maintain legitimate peripheral participation as they develop their identities in practice. The community of practice (Wenger, 1998) within the context of a classroom is one in which the practices shaped by the culture of the classroom determine how learning is defined, instructed, and practiced. Patterns of social interaction such as discourse, organizational practices, and sanctioned activities and routines foster shared understandings about meanings, forms, and uses of learning (Turner, 1995). Student agency, within this context, is co-constructed as students continually interpret and improvise within such settings.

From this theoretical stance, teachers and students share the instructional floor; and pivotal to this understanding and view of agency is how interactions, perceptions, and learning spaces are structures that influence access to agency. Opportunities for students to use self-directed symbolizations and improvisation (referenced in Chapter 2) as tools to enact their agency provide the necessary supports that facilitate access to student's agency.

We must acknowledge that in unpacking each of the dimensions of agency, one can get lost in focusing on each dimension individually (i.e., intentionality, purpose, persistence, perception) without paying close attention to how these dimensions work in unison or in how learning environments envelop these dimensions. Further discussion about how each of these dimensions intersect in classrooms and schools is addressed in Part II, Chapters 7 and 8. However, within each of these dimensions of agency, a core understanding is that students are situated in complex communities of practice where students, schools, structures, opportunities, and interactions shape one's ability to harness and act on their agency.

For student agency to exist in schools, at the heart, teachers and students must share the instructional floor. Teachers are central in how students develop their identities and how they are positioned in their roles as learners and agentic individuals. Students must value what it is they are doing, persist, and continue with the tasks set forth to accomplish what it is they want to do in relation to their ideas and intentions. As students must also be willing to wrestle with their ideas when it comes to acting with agency, teachers can support students' agency by structuring learning environments and events supportive of student agency.

What can teachers do to listen and support students' ideas, intentions, and their purpose for what it is they want to accomplish? Consider these compelling narratives from classrooms where teachers co-constructed projects and modeled to students how these central dimensions of agency (perception and persistence) coincided.

Barton et al. (2008) describe how during science learning activities students can construct new identities and learning capabilities. In their description of Amelia, a middle school student, often termed "troublemaker" in the class, through the activities structured in the class and the support of her teacher, who guided and extended her thinking, and her participation in science-related activities, Amelia was able to take up the identity of a student who was interested in science and who had power and agency in her work. During the unit, Amelia navigated her identity as an individual who was interested and knowledgeable about the topic of worms. She valued what she was doing and in the process of engaging meaningfully in the community, she developed a deep sense of agency in her work as a scientist. "What one is able to do in a setting is dialectically related to what one can access and activate in that setting, and that includes an understanding of content or of rules for participation" (Barton et al., 2008, p. 75).

The power of constructing agentic opportunities with students where they are perceived as knowledgeable meaning-makers requires thoughtful and careful planning. In my collaborative research with Indigenous teachers, who teach in an elementary school with a high percentage of Native American students, teachers implement culturally relevant practices to structure activities for students to share their voice and stories. Within this teacher inquiry group, the teachers continually interrogate and critically analyze their practices. They share their reflections about the lack of opportunities for Indigenous students' voices and stories in the curriculum.

> After we met during our teacher meeting [inquiry group session], I took my kids down to the library and said, "Where are the books written by our people? You know, by us, authors from our Tribe? That's you guys." You know that really became my vision after I heard that. My vision is for my kids to be authors-real writers. I just kept those words . . . they just kept coming back to me. There are no Native authors from our Tribe down there in that library, and they're [my students] going to be some of the first. So, that was exciting to me. I was going to do a collaborative lesson with students. My kids were going to be one of the first authors in our library from our Tribe. We're going to make books with this curriculum we're all doing. (Vaughn, 2016, p. 35)

Like Yolie, the teachers in the inquiry group developed rich units of study with the culminating activity of a class dual language book in the Tribe's language and in English. The teachers recognized the opening in the curriculum that would allow for their Native students to have agency and be successful in literacy if afforded the opportunity to learn within a curriculum that responded to students' cultures, identities, and strengths. For example, Brianna shared, "It's important for us to do this [develop this curriculum], not only for them to become better writers, but just with Native students, that they have a way to express themselves. And so it's something that we really have to work on, for them to be able to say that's me, I'm here and to be able to communicate what their thinking, and how they feel" (Vaughn, 2016, p. 36).

Continually, we see exciting research like this, where teachers engage in thoughtful and reflective practice to support students' linguistic, racial, and cultural backgrounds. For example, Campano (2007) who in his teacher research structured classroom learning experiences with his students where they could explore and craft narratives out of their family refugee experiences, structured learning events meaningful and relevant to students' lives. In doing so, spaces to listen and honor students were forged. He shared the following:

> It was striking to me how Priscilla's and Ma-Lee's survival stories were also ineluctably educational narratives. What I found most moving was that all these children, although from different backgrounds, asserted their deep emotional investment in schooling. . . . The children's growth in my class was at least partially predicated on our ability to create a classroom community that would encourage them to recognize the value of their own experiences. (pp. 68–69)

Like Yolie and Brianna, Campano examined his practice and directed his planning with a focus on students' critical experiences. As these classrooms suggest, participatory structures are necessary to provide spaces for students to harness their agency in classrooms. Understanding how motivational dimensions underlie student agency is critical in discussing how teachers can structure activities alongside their students while cultivating tasks and activities where students value what it is they are learning, believe that they can pursue their ideas and tasks related to their intentions, and persist as needed to pursue their ideas.

EXTENSION

At the core of student agency is understanding that agency is a collective process and is not solely dependent on students or teachers and schools. Understanding how systematic structures in schools have marginalized students of color and from nondominant backgrounds is vital.

1. What are some ways that schools can invite students, parents/ guardians, community members, and other stakeholders into the classroom? How can we encourage a more inclusive and culturally responsive approach to the types of tasks and activities we structure in schools to afford more opportunities for student agency?

2. As students are more driven to learn when they set their own paths for what it is they want to learn, understanding what their perceptions of the activities they do is essential. Engage in conversations with students about the tasks they do in class. Ask them to share if these activities and tasks have value to them. What are strategies they engage in when they have obstacles that allow them to persist?

CHAPTER 4

Interaction and Negotiation

Teaching is not simply about reading, or math or art. Instead, it is also about who is heard, listened to, and read, who gets to count, and who can paint the picture. It's about who moves ahead and who gets left behind. In this sense, teaching is political work, and it has always been so.

—Sonia Nieto (2006, p. 23)

Understanding how students interact and negotiate their agency in spaces and how spaces are structured in schools greatly informs an understanding of student agency. Students do not merely act with agency; they engage in activities, use resources and tools; and interact and negotiate their identities and participation in these complex social contexts alongside peers and their teacher. Teachers and peers can facilitate agency or impede students in their efforts to develop their agency. Students' positionality informs this layer of agency. Using the theoretical lens of smartness (Hatt, 2007, 2012), interactions and negotiation underlie how students interact and participate in these complex spaces.

INTERACTION

How students position themselves and are positioned in classroom spaces affects their ability to influence, alter, and expand opportunities within their context. Agency cannot be solely conceptualized at the individual level as students position themselves and are positioned in classrooms that can either support or detract from their ability to exert influence and act with agency. As we think about how students are positioned in schools, we need to recognize that schools are traditionally competitive and have historically marginalized students of color and those from nondominant cultures. Schools continue to afford access for some to exert their agency while leaving others behind.

Think back to Mae, a White, female, in Chapter 3 who decided to pursue the lunch recycling program after observing the waste produced at lunch at her school. Mae's teacher was supportive but was told she needed to get approval from the student council and that her idea needed their support. Persisting had much to do with her efforts as she met monthly with the student council, but to fully understand how such an act occurred, let's examine Mae's identity and position in the context of her class and school. Positionality affords access for students to interact and negotiate their ideas in schools. In her 4th-grade class, Mae was positioned as someone who was "smart" by her teacher and her peers.

> Smartness is culturally produced . . . but made "real" through discourse and tangible artifacts such as grades, standardized test scores, entry to gifted programs, and academic credentials. Such artifacts become connected to and underlie students' academic identities, influenc[ing] students' perceptions of themselves and their own abilities over time. (Hatt, 2012, p. 455)

Classroom practices supported Mae's identity as someone who was smart. Each week, students had reading goals deemed by in-class and out-of-school reading time and points they received on a computerized reading program. Her teacher, Mrs. Hill, posted the points students read from tests on the computerized reading program on the whiteboard in front of the class. I was a researcher in this classroom and conducted afterschool book clubs with students in Mrs. Hill's class and the neighboring 3rd and 5th-grade classes. One afternoon a parent came in and complained about the public display of points and how such a reward system humiliated their child and other students who didn't receive the "right" score. Mrs. Hill defended her practice and shared that, in fact, the parent was wrong and that posting the points motivated her students. The parent went on to complain to the principal, but since the computerized reading program was used throughout the district, the principal shared that this was not something she alone could change. In Mrs. Hill's class, this public display became an artifact of both student and teachers' interpretations of smartness. Mae's name was on the board each week that I observed, whereas other students' names were not. This classroom structure instilled competitiveness and those who were deemed as smart had access to do extracurricular things.

For example, another key artifact that served as an interpretation of smartness in Mrs. Hill's 4th-grade classroom was being sent to volunteer as a kindergarten helper. Being sent to another class to be a teacher helper was a special job only given to students who completed their work, were compliant, and who Mrs. Hill deemed would be helpful to her colleague in kindergarten. Mae was sent to kindergarten each day to volunteer at the end of the day. In addition, Mae was given entry to the school's gifted program. Students' identities as being smart or a troublemaker are conceptualized through artifacts, interactions, and dialogue like this. Without understanding the social context and the ways in which students are positioned in schools, we may be tempted to see student agency as solely inherent or something individuals have or don't have. For example, Mae had agency in her pursuits, but her position in her classroom and school greatly contributed to her ability to pursue her ideas and thereby harness agency.

Contrast this to Mae's classmate, James, a student whom Mrs. Hill deemed a troublemaker. James could often be found in the classroom at recess as a form of punishment (at least on the days when I would conduct research, one time a week over the school year). James was never sent to the kindergarten class to help out or given access to the gifted program, which at the time just accepted teacher referrals for entry to the program. James's name was rarely on the whiteboard for meeting the reading award points set forth by Mrs. Hill. It's hard to suppose what might have happened if James had proposed the lunch recycling program over Mae, but given that James had such limited access in the classroom it's doubtful that he would feel comfortable to share his ideas and that his ideas would have been as widely accepted. Students' agency is inextricably linked to their identities of who is considered smart.

NEGOTIATION

Smartness informs our discussion about student agency because it helps to contextualize who in schools has "valuable knowledge" (Tyack & Cuban, 1997), which students' voices and opinions are listened to and supported, and who has negotiation power. Critical scholars emphasize how schools have long marginalized students of color and students from homes where English is not the primary language (Flores, 2016; Mariscal et al., 2017). The hidden curriculum "consists of the implicit messages given to students about differential power and social evaluation as they learn how to work in schools, what kinds of knowledge exists . . . and how students are valued in their own right" (de Marrais & LeCompte, 1995, p. 207). As Hatt (2012) states, "What is taught in schools includes who 'is' and 'is not' smart and what smartness means. Determinations are based on teachers' expectations mediated by knowledge of students' socioeconomic backgrounds and racial identities" (p. 457). When we think about student agency, we must critically analyze who has access and who is deemed smart and how such identities allow for teachers and schools to provide opportunities for some to use their agency while leaving others out. Students develop identities as those capable of exerting their influence and position as part of this cultural production of what it means to be smart in their classroom.

Adding to this complexity is the recent pressures of standardized assessments. Over the last 30 years in the United States, there has been exponential growth in federal and state oversight in education. Restrictive policies and pay-for-performance measures have driven schools to ensure student achievement on standardized assessments, leaving opportunities for student agency behind. Because many educators across the nation face enormous challenges and pressures to adhere to district-wide mandates to improve student performance on standardized assessments, schools may further exacerbate who is and who isn't smart and whose voice matters during instruction. Teachers in schools are not to blame. While it is true that teachers have the immediate influence of their classrooms, to look at teachers as the sole reason as to why agency has not been widely adopted in schools "would be convenient but misleading" (Wortham, 2006, p. 26). Processes such as larger educational discourse at the federal, state, and local district level greatly inform how such opportunities may or may not be practiced in classrooms.

Teachers are pressured by pay-for-performance measures to teach to a "one-size-fits-all" approach, especially in core subjects that are tested (reading and mathematics), but this type of instruction is based on teaching that "is not changing the trajectory of the very students for whom the mandates have been put in place" (Brenner & Hiebert, 2010, p. 361). This drive to increase student achievement to receive federal funding pressures administrators and teachers to meet student achievement goals, which leaves little room for instructional opportunities for student agency.

However, research has supported the claim that student agency is an important dimension of effective student learning (Ivey & Johnston, 2013; Johnston et al., 2016). Findings of exemplary 1st-and 4th-grade teachers revealed that effective teachers developed learning environments where students were autonomous decisionmakers (Pressley et al., 2001). In these exemplary classrooms, "the most effective teachers did more to encourage students to do things for themselves than did least effective teachers" (p. 17). These exemplary teachers viewed learning as a co-constructed process, facilitating learning opportunities so that students could take control of their own learning pursuits (Vaughn, Premo et al., 2020). Similarly, Johnston (2004) emphasized the role of teachers in their ability to support student agency:

> Teachers' conversations with children help the children build the bridges between action and consequences that develop their sense of agency. They show children how, by acting strategically, they accomplish things, and at the same time, that they are the kind of person who accomplishes things. (p. 30)

By opening the curriculum to students' interests and inquiries, teachers have the ability to use language and resources to codevelop a collaborative space with their students. When teachers and schools recognize students' interests and backgrounds, they orient their approach to classroom instruction and develop meaningful tasks with their students. These collaborative spaces provide rich contexts for student learning and student agency.

Within the classroom context, student agency is interdependent and mediated by teachers, other learners, and the individual's actions and intentions during learning situations. Within this socially mediated view, individuals are collectively and individually shaped by their participation and nonparticipation during literacy practices. Hilppö et al. (2016) emphasize how agency is socially constructed [and] how individuals position and are positioned.

> We regard sense of agency not solely as something people feel or provide a narrative account of, but also as something people invoke, or choose not to invoke, in certain situations. In sum, a sense of agency can be viewed] as a socially constructed relation between an individual's capabilities, aspirations, and perceived opportunities and limitations to take action with a given practice. (p. 51)

In this way, agency is socially constructed as students engage in different practices and in complex learning and social environments to develop their agency. Thus, student agency is multidimensional and functions as a jointly constructed action. For example, a student in the midst of adopting an agentic stance takes action individually or with others in a deliberate manner to make alternative decisions that are central to the practice of the classroom. Although the teacher structures specific activities for students during learning experiences, the learners are active participants, acting on and within the instructional situation. Student agency flourishes when school activities, materials, and structures afford students freedom to (1) make significant decisions about their learning, (2) voice their opinions about issues that matter to them, and (3) challenge what they're taught, especially if their background equips them with a competing perspective.

Across disciplines and contexts, research highlights how students' interactions and negotiations affect their agency and how teachers can help to construct such opportunities. Curricula reform efforts to afford students access and the ability to share their voice is instrumental in these efforts. In my research with teachers, many teachers engaged in a pedagogical re-envisioning to structure opportunities for student agency, veering away from prescribed curricula, where students' cultures, language, and backgrounds were positioned as valuable knowledge in the curriculum.

Kayla shared during an interview, "I'm taking what I know about the Writing Workshop and then making it all about how culture can be the main thing in writing" (personal communication, June 15, 2013). Like Kayla, teachers infused the curriculum with culturally responsive resources from their shared experiences as Native educators, understandings of Native culture, stories told by Tribal Elders, and critical discussions about the role and function of writing (e.g., where are Native voices about topics and issues central to students' lives). Consider the following reflection from Yolie where she described how she used Native stories to talk about animal characteristics with her students.

> I tried to use the stories as the anchor texts for the mini-lessons. This [anchor text] is something we use during the Writing Workshop, but I was telling stories instead of using actual books about the animals and asking them questions like, "What do you already know about Hummingbird and how Hummingbird tries to help Coyote?" instead of using the more traditional kinds of books. Talking about the stories helps them [students] dig deeper. (personal communication, June 17, 2013)

Using oral stories to discuss animal characteristics rather than using "more traditional kinds of books" provided an opportunity for Yolie's students to dig deeper as a way to make Native culture central in Yolie's writing instruction. Yolie further shared, "If they can relate something to their own lives like the stories and make personal connections, they're more likely to want to do this [writing]" (personal communication, June 17, 2013). In this way, rather than using more traditional texts as anchor texts, Yolie re-envisioned the workshop model to include oral storytelling as a way to support her students and to make cultural ties to the curriculum.

These experiences of re-envisioning the curriculum to counter the constraints of the restrictive approaches to teaching reading and writing emphasized in their school highlights how teachers can structure opportunities centered on student agency and cultivate spaces for students to be able to negotiate and interact on their behalf. Consider Kayla's reflection during another interview about the schoolwide team's reactions to give more attention to Native culture in the writing curriculum: "Tying cultural relevancy into the Writing Workshop has influenced my thinking because we're doing writing a different way—it's really a different way of writing instruction" (personal communication, April 19, 2013). She further shared,

> Now when I'm doing the lesson I am always thinking of ways to bring the culture in. I am really trying to tie it—if I am selecting materials for my classroom, I am trying to make that cultural connection, always. Me, because being Native American and it's kind of there for me, always, like I see it. (personal communication, May 4, 2013)

Such reflection emphasizes how teachers' racialized identities inform the ways in which they approach their teaching. Kayla described developing a poetry unit relating the seasons to important cultural activities and resources as a way to support her and her student's identities as Native Americans (Vaughn, 2016).

Providing contexts where teachers embed students' linguistic, cultural, and racial identities into practice is essential in understanding how to structure agentic opportunities. Edwards and D'Arcy (2004), for example, describe how student agency was embedded in curricular activities, highlighting students' linguistic abilities. In their research of 31 middle school bilingual students who were invited to teach their native language to student teachers, the students were positioned as knowledgeable learners and meaning-makers who were supported in their efforts to demonstrate their knowledge and agency and share their ideas. Students' languages were varied (e.g., Arabic, Bengali, Bosnian, Chinese, Cre´ole, Kurdish, Punjabi, Serbian, Somalian, Thai, and Urdu). The traditional teacher as all-knowing was flipped in this learning environment where "the traditional power dynamics of the classroom were disturbed and . . . [where] a fresh learning zone had been created where there was more freedom of movement for learners and teachers and new pathways of participation available" (Edwards & D'Arcy, 2004, p. 153).

Similarly, consider how two 5th-grade students harnessed their agency in their mathematics class (Brown, 2009). Opportunities for agency can occur when teachers help to structure flexible and supportive environments that position students as agentic. Brown (2009) described Kim and Tanya, two female students who initially viewed mathematics in terms of facts and procedures but eventually perceived mathematics in terms of conceptual understanding and as a conduit for enacting their agency. These students were able to act with agency, that is "in terms of their capacity to offer support and to seek support from others" (Edwards & Mackenzie, 2005).

Garcia et al. (2015) describe the development of agency among high school students in their productions of important topics in their local community through the development of digital productions. As part of an action research program in which high school students research and create multimedia presentations about topics important to them, high school students leveraged their agency and demonstrated sophisticated understandings of sociopolitical topics. These high school students were invited to the American Educational Research Association (AERA) to share their productions. Students were positioned as knowledgeable and resourceful in their development of their action research projects and in their presentation at the international research conference, which further cultivated a sense of agency in their roles as knowledgeable learners and agentic students.

> The trip to New Orleans was an experience that changes a person. I never thought I could be such a revolutionary, but an experience like AERA tells me that I have a future in this field. It tells me that I am not someone that will sit around and take oppression; I am someone who will be an advocate for change. After listening to educators and administrators applaud us on our work, I realized that I can make a change. (Garcia et al., 2015, p. 164)

Other opportunities for agency can be seen with even younger students. Dyson (1997), in her research of 2nd- and 3rd-grade students, Holly and Tina, used writing as a tool to reference their own agency in discussing superheroes with their peers and teacher. Specifically, Tina "reconstructed relations, making new selections from available possibilities—negating, extending, foregrounding, and recombing them [characters] in new ways" (Dyson, 1997, p. 112). Classroom structures were flexible to afford opportunities for students to play around with materials and resources to exert their agency. Students were positioned as knowledgeable, and they negotiated their ideas and interests in their writing pursuits.

When schools provide space and resources to support students' ideas, projects, and interest, spaces for agency are cultivated. Classroom structures and supports afford opportunities for students to interact and negotiate their agency in classrooms and schools. Understanding how students are positioned and the ways in which spaces are structured in schools underlies how to cultivate student agency. Students engage and disengage in activities using available resources and tools and negotiate their agency during social interactions. The ways in which students are positioned as smart and knowledgeable affords access to enacting agency in these complex spaces.

In describing positionality as a core tenet of student agency, negotiation and interaction emphasize that agentic identities are fluid and shifting and change continually in classrooms. Agency is not reliant solely on the individual but is rather connected to others, materials, resources, and the historical institution of schooling. Envisioning the institution of schooling as a place for student agency requires that we interrogate how students are positioned in learning spaces, especially for those historically marginalized in schools, and ensure that all stakeholders are critical and reflective of practices to afford equitable learning spaces where all voices are not only heard but included.

EXTENSION

Student agency is deeply embedded in the structures that afford students freedom to (1) make significant decisions about their learning; (2) voice their opinions about issues that matter to them, and (3) challenge what they're taught.

1. Reflect on what existing structures and supports are in place that allow for students to engage in these practices in schools.
2. Reflect on what existing structures and supports are in place that allow for students of color and from nondominant backgrounds to engage in these practices in schools.

3. What are the differences between your responses to questions 1 and 2? Write a letter to your principal outlining these differences and suggestions of how to re-envision the inequities you see.

4. Critically examine the idea of smartness in schools. How has the concept of smartness further marginalized students in today's current educational context? Think of this either locally, statewide, nationally, or globally. What are some strategies and practices that educators can engage in to cultivate more equitable spaces to challenge the concept of smartness in schools? What would result for students' agency?

Part II

GROWING STUDENT AGENCY

CHAPTER 5

How Students Experience and Talk About Agency

I think a way to support agency in schools would be to just talk to students, hear them out.

—9th-grader, female

The demands on teachers are increasingly challenging, with increased pay-for-performance pressures and a heightened emphasis on standards to student performance. There are so many things to consider, from meeting the latest district requirements to following up with parents, to conducting the latest assessment and meeting the requirements set forward by grade-level teams. It is not always feasible nor easy to sit and talk with students about their ideas, interests, and perspectives about what it is they are doing. However, one of the most valuable things was when I sat next to my students and asked them about school. At the time, I wasn't necessarily focused on agency but more on how to provide engaging opportunities for my students during reading. After a few discussions, I realized that some of the activities in the classroom were more widely accessible and interesting to students than others. Students shared with me their opinions that made me reflect on my practices:

- I liked it [reading] but it's just that the chapter books are so long and it annoys me when it gets old—I always get chapter books though because I can read like that.
- My most favorite thing about reading in the room is the reading center. I like this because you get to choose a book in that center, but see in the topic baskets and the Drop Everything and Read (DEAR) bag, the teacher picks out the books. In the reading center, it has all kinds of books that we could pick.

- I really don't like Calendar; it's so boring.
- My favorite part of reading in the classroom is the reading center because it has lots of books, and lots of details and there are books up there by students in the reading center. We made books and we made reading books; a lot of time we publish our books and then we after took them home. I published a lot of books—the pumpkin, the fuzzy bear. We get to read our books.
- I love reading that with a buddy because you get to share time and spend time with a buddy and you get to do fun stuff with your buddy.
- My favorite center was called, RAT (Read Anything). It isn't really a center but I really like it because you could read anything, even Leapfrog; you could read it without the headphones if you wanted to. Sometimes you can read it out loud and then put the things down and read other things— anything that are books and including the books on the board—anything that had reading in it, any centers—anything with books. I really like the reading center. I tried to skip the other work so I could just go and read.

These students' reflections about our classroom made me think differently about my practice. My students had specific ideas, interests, and understandings about reading and how it was being taught in the classroom than what I thought. For instance, why not abandon doing calendar, since many of the students I talked with shared the same sentiment ("it's so boring")? Why not have students pick out their reading books for topic baskets, and why not provide students with opportunities to choose how they wanted to read (with a partner, by themselves, using technology, etc.)? Regrettably, asking students their thoughts about classroom activities was something I hadn't considered before these discussions. But, after listening to my students, I realized that in order to make my practice more equitable, it was imperative to listen to my students and hear what they had to say about their experiences.

For schools to support students and their agency, understanding what students think and have to say about their experiences is essential. Students have a powerful voice in what they say and do and how classroom practices should be structured to support their agency. Repeatedly, scholars demonstrate the important role of student voice in the structuring of classroom practices and learning opportunities (e.g., Dyson, 2020; Mayes et al., 2017; Quinn & Owen, 2016). Students of all ages can provide insight into what they are learning, how they are learning, and whether their learning environment supports their ideas and decisions—and ultimately their agency.

Bakhtin's (1981) notion of dialogism provides a lens for examining students' perspectives about agency, the ways in which agency is intertwined in complex learning communities, and the ideological views of how agency informs classroom practices. Accordingly, the work of Bakhtin (1986) situates a theory of voice within the active, situated, and functional nature of speech as it is employed by various communities (such as classrooms) within a particular society (e.g., a school).

Bakhtin (1981) maintained that "in dialogue with others, people give personal voice to utterances that are imbued with the meanings, intentions, and accents of past and present contexts of use" (p. 293). From a Bakhtinian perspective, voice can be considered any form of spoken, written or nonverbal communication, which is a link in a chain of communication. Within this chain of communication, the speaking personality of a student or teacher is inherently related to the voices of others (teachers and students, past or present). In other words, students are part of a complex, social context where they use their voice, materials, and resources to express their interests, desires, and motivations. Thus, it is essential to listen to and consider students' perspectives about school practices in order to have an understanding of how student agency can have a role in schoolwide practices. What does agency mean from those who experience schooling directly? I recently set out to ask students about their agency in schools, what it means to them, their experiences with feeling agentic in school, and any thoughts on what could be done to support their agency in school. I highlight these important responses from students and provide compelling classroom-based insight from my research as well as from those of other scholars to provide a backdrop of how students experience their agency in classroom contexts.

WHAT DO STUDENTS HAVE TO SAY ABOUT AGENCY?

When talking with students about their agency in schools, students emphasized the power of possessing a voice and having a choice in their roles as learners. In instances where students felt as though they had agency, they were positioned as knowledgeable decisionmakers and individuals capable of exerting influence in their learning contexts. Importantly, students from across grades expressed ideas about their agency in school. Consider the following responses from students when asked what agency means to them.

VOICE AND CHOICE

Agency Means . . .

"Agency means having a choice and letting my ideas be heard to do what I'm interested in."—5th-grader, female

"To me, as a student, agency means that I get to have a say in my education. It allows me to voice my opinion on what I want learn, and how I want learn it. Everyone has their own way of doing things, no matter what it is, me included. By giving students a choice, it allows them to discover and use the way they learn the best way they can."—7th-grader, female

"Having a voice in school."—10th-grader, male

"Agency means that I have a voice in my learning for the future."—12th-grader, female

"Having a voice in what I want to learn about in school and the way I learn it."—11th-grader, female

"Agency means to have kids have a choice and to be able to have their say in what they want and can do in the classroom."—4th-grader, female

"It means to have a say in what you do."—6th-grader, female

"Agency as a student to me feels like free speech and a say at what happens in school."—8th-grader, male

"Having a voice as a student would certainly make me feel more involved in school and more valued."—9th-grader, male

"Having agency as a student means quite a lot. You can have a part and voice in your own education, with guidance. It's important to take part in your learning, not wait for others to do it for you."—6th-grader, female

"Being able to decide things as a whole school by possibly voting or being able to choose your classes."—6th-grader, male

"It means being able to choose what my day will look like and what type of activities I would prefer to do in school. It would be being able to choose what kind of learning I want to do, whether that's online, reading from books, lectures, hands on, or more."—7th-grader, female

"It means being able to freely say your opinions to others to help improve something. In this case maybe the school system or rules made in school."—3rd-grader, male

"As a student, having agency would make me feel that grade school will help me learn more about what I want to become after high school even if the classes only cover the basics. I still feel that schools should require students to take classes from a variety of subjects, especially in earlier grades to help students branch out and see what they enjoy." —8th-grader, male

These powerful insights provide a compelling tone for what student agency is and could be. By inviting students' voices about their experiences and wonderings, schools can begin to rethink how to structure activities conducive to student agency. One tangible way to invite students' voice into schooling practices and thereby support their agency is to have conversations with students like those quoted. Additionally, schools can engage in participatory action research, a process by which students become integral researchers, observers, and change agents through collective decisionmaking. Participatory action research supports an approach of fostering collective agency in students by inviting students and communities to understand and take action toward community change (Cook-Sather, 2020). Positive outcomes result when students are viewed as collaborators in constructing agency in schools. For example, Ferguson et al. (2011) shared how through participatory action research students were able to have more dialogue about the decisionmaking process in the school and teachers saw how to structure activities where students could have more agency.

Teachers committed themselves to embedding more choices into and after the school day and making those choices clearer to students, conducting social skills lessons around specific topics, and developing effective learning groups. Teachers were also interested in continuing to elicit input from students and therefore shared that they would ask for feedback, provide more opportunities for students to express themselves, and work to build better relationship with their students. (Ferguson et al., 2011, p. 68)

Like this practice, schools can deliberately engage in inviting students' voices and feedback about activities and opportunities for agency through practical strategies and schoolwide structures. Brasof and Spector (2016), for example, describe how schoolwide practices can be centered on student voice and agency by adopting a belief system embedded in student participation and civic engagement. School personnel were able to review their underlying principles, beliefs, and norms and developed a belief system focused on fostering student voice and a schoolwide civic culture. Such research highlights that through incorporating opportunities for students to share their voice in the curriculum and schoolwide structures and practices, spaces for agency can be cultivated.

Knowledgeable Decisionmakers

Interestingly, students provided insight into how specific school structures and relationships with teachers and administrators supported their sense of agency. Consider how students' responses about being positioned as knowledgeable decisionmakers afforded opportunities to feel a sense of agency.

"When I was in 6th grade one of my connections classes was STEM. At the end of the semester, everyone in the class had to complete a Capstone project. The main instructions were to make any sort of presentation about something you enjoy, and talk about how it relates to science, technology, engineering, art, and/or math. In this particular project we were able to choose our own topic, and how we would present it. I liked this assignment because it gave students the opportunity to make decisions on their own. I ended up making a Google Slides presentation about music, and guitars, and how they relate to science, technology, and art. My STEM teacher really liked project and enjoyed my presentation. Many of the other projects were very good as well, but each one was unique, because we had the freedom to make our own decisions."—7th-grader, female

"I think having agency as a student means a lot about the level of trust between me and school administration and teachers. A way that almost all high school students at my high school are able to experience a sense of agency is through our open campus policy for lunch; we are free to go wherever, either on campus or off campus, and are expected to be back to the school by our next class period. I think that this one part of my day allows me to truly feel independent, which also makes me feel empowered, and because our administration and staff allows us this freedom, I think it makes me feel more understanding about other issues that they cannot be as lenient about. Another more niche way in which a lot of students, including myself, experience agency is through a class at the high school called Extended Learning Internship (ELI) in which we choose a topic to study in depth for a semester, and essentially initiate all of the research and associated tasks ourselves. This project has made me feel like a mini-adult and well respected by my peers, and a good deal of that respect comes with the freedom and trust that I am granted to work on such an intensive project (as a senior thesis might be to a college student) by myself. Of course, we have a supervisor who keeps us on track, but her job is relatively hands-off. In that sense, I think that having agency as a student has really allowed me to come into myself in a buffered way; I have the opportunities to take hold of parts of my education, but I also still have the choice to just go with the flow before I am thrown into the more serious world. Having agency as a student feels like good life practice to me."—11th-grader, female

When students are viewed as knowledgeable decisionmakers, they have the potential to exert influence in their environment and pursue their intentions and ideas. For example, Campano et al. (2013), in their research of a public charter school comprised of a 99% African American student population, documented how, through schoolwide practices and critical literacy instruction, students were viewed as knowledgeable decisionmakers as, "advocates for others. . . . and as role models that could inspire others' life opportunities" (p. 118). Similarly, Keiler (2018) in her research of two urban high schools documented how students took an active role in the learning process rather than being passive in a student-centered STEM instructional program. Students became empowered as they made decisions to support their learning and ideas and enacted their agency throughout the learning environment to engage in science learning. Viewing students as knowledgeable decisionmakers provides compelling evidence about how teachers and schools can view students in ways that support their sense of agency.

Do Students Feel They Have Opportunities to Make Choices and Share Their Voice?

Given that choice and voice were an important aspect of what students believed was central to student agency, I asked students to share opportunities in schools and in their classrooms where they made choices and shared their voice. Interestingly, students shared minimal opportunities where they made choices and shared their voice. Responses ranged from none at all to describing activities outside of school.

> "I don't feel like I have a lot of choice. She usually has a plan for the day and it doesn't change—we can't change it."—4th-grader, female

> "I have almost none—no choice at all."—7th-grader, female

> "I feel I do not have much choice as a student because I am almost never given an option but a command."—8th-grader, male

> "In some of my clubs, such as National Honor Society and Beta Club, but other than that I feel as if I have had no voice in my school."—11th-grade, female

> "I feel like I have no freedom to choose."—11th-grade, female

> "Somewhat, but not enough. I think I can freely voice my opinion, but it will never make a change."—12th-grade, female

> "Little, to none. I feel everything is pretty set to a schedule that we must follow with the exception of every couple teachers that are a little more loose."—12th-grade, male

> "I don't think I have that many choices. A lot of my classes have a feel of just putting my head down and working, but I also don't really know how else some of those classes would get across the same important information if I were to choose or make decisions."—8th-grader, male

> "This [having choice] is very rare and only happened to me once. It happened last year in geometry class. My class breezed through the material by late March, so the teacher asked my class if we wanted to learn some algebra II stuff so we could get a head start on it the following year. We agreed to do it. Apart from that, teachers decide with the other teachers in the department what they will teach the students."—9th-grader, male

Do Students Feel That School Provides Them with Opportunities to Be Viewed as Knowledgeable Decisionmakers?

I asked explicitly of a specific example or experience at school where they had an idea about a project, pursued this idea, and made decisions about what they were doing. The following responses highlight where these opportunities occurred. There were two common subject areas, writing and social studies, where students shared that they had such opportunities.

"Well, in opinion writing we get to choose our own opinion and write about it but the teacher gives us the topic."—4th-grader, female

"Sometimes in writing we get to choose what we do our debating topic on. We will either pick a controversial topic or choose one side of an argument that the teacher prepares for us, but the teachers are always supportive no matter what topic we pick."—6th-grader, male

"In social studies, we are given a topic to study. Then within this topic, I was given a smaller topic to study, so no, I guess I didn't really make any choices there."—4th-grader, male

"I feel like we have more agency in writing and social studies mostly because we are always doing individual topics."—8th-grader, male

"All of the subjects are presented in the same way in my school. Listen to a lecture, take notes, take a quiz, then hear more lectures, then take a unit test."—8th-grader, female

"I think I have more choice in my gifted class, my social studies class, and my language arts class. We have more projects in those classes and I can more often than not choose what I would like to research about or write about."—7th-grader, male

"I have never had an idea about a project that I pursued in school, so I can't really answer this question well. All my projects are outside of school."—9th-grader, male

"In science class we had a semester-long assignment that just ended up being extra credit if you did it; it was called the 20% time project. Basically what it was, was something to fill your free time with in class; people just choose whatever assignment they want to do (make it up) and they do it. It had to be related to chemistry, however. I did a research paper on how engineering was used in science."—11th-grader, female

"One time in English we were doing a project about the civil rights movement and our teacher said if we could come up with our own idea. I told her my idea, which was a movie trailer. She said this would fit the criteria, so I did it. I finished the project and presented. When she graded it she said my idea wasn't a good fit for the project. I felt cheated and I was frustrated because I tried to be creative and I felt punished."
—8th-grade, male

"I really can't remember any times."—11th-grader, female

"There has hardly ever been a time like this. I am quiet most the time and don't always like to voice my opinion. The only time I can think of is senior project where we picked a topic to research, and even then there were quite a bit of restrictions."—10th-grader, female

"For my agricultural science class I had to come up with a project that used what we had learned in class. I made a garden for my mom. I went to Lowe's and got all the stuff and then created the garden, mainly herbs and tomatoes. My parents were really supportive but the teacher wasn't really. It was stressful."—9th-grader, female

"Most projects that we are given are planned out and we have to do it in a specific way, whether we like the idea or not."—8th-grader, male

"I really have no idea of a time I did this at school."—7th-grader, female

If we think about the substantial reform that is needed to embed student agency into schools, important insights can be drawn from these responses. Overwhelmingly, students felt as though they had limited opportunities for choice and decisionmaking except for an accelerated class, an add-on capstone project, or perhaps in selecting a writing prompt or a social studies topic to pursue. All these opportunities are valid as opportunities for supporting student agency, but they also highlight the sad state of student agency in these schools. Unfortunately, students viewed having a agency as distant and elusive in their day-to-day interactions in school.

Interestingly, much like with conversations with my 1st-graders many years ago, many of the students I spoke with had specific ideas about schooling—from providing direction on what it is they want to learn to thinking about their choice and decisionmaking around pursuing activities and how they were positioned in their classroom. In short, students shared valuable insight on the integral dimensions of agency:

- Dispositional: Intentionality and purpose—what it is that students want to learn and why and specific ideas about what they want to learn.
- Motivational: Perception and persistence—students' thoughts about the types of tasks they are doing and whether they want to pursue them.
- Positional: Interaction and negotiation—How are learning opportunities positioning students? Who are viewed as

knowledgeable and smart and who has access to learning opportunities as a result?

In fact, conversations with students revealed how each of these dimensions manifested (and did not manifest) in their classrooms.

> "I never even tried to ask about doing a project or something I am interested in. I know my teacher would think I was distracting her and the class and I would get into trouble for doing that in class."—8th-grader, male

> "I would like the choice of skipping the reward parties to read in the library. For me, agency means embarrassing myself or maybe annoying the teacher . . . and I don't really want to do that."—5th-grader, female

> "One thing in my class is that the teacher just sets it up like it's all about whose smart and whose not. If you are one of the kids who gets the answer right all the time and if you make just 1 mistake you are then viewed as dumb and it's so much pressure."—4th-grader, female

> "My favorite subject is math. In math we do math problems fast. It would be great if we could do things we were interested in like real stuff. Well the thing is, it would be great because then it would be like they [the teachers] were helping you. Like they could ask you what do you want to do, as a profession? And they could help you work toward that and get a start on that. And that would just be great knowing with that, that your teachers are here to support you and that they're here to help you through stuff you, but that usually doesn't happen."—5th-grader, female

> "Because I'm one of the readers who can read, I go out in the hallway and use the computers to do my research project. The teacher doesn't work with me and the other kids. We work on our own. The rest of the kids are in the classroom hearing what the teacher says."—3rd-grader, male

A critical look at these responses suggests the students' thoughtfulness and insight about schooling. Students were fully aware of the many structural inequalities, ranging from the constraints of curricular programs adopted in their schools to the inequities of tracking that positioned and too often limited not only their ability to choose but their classmates' ability as well. These eloquent responses from students provide critical evaluation of the inequities students experience, which not only impede their sense of agency but continue to call attention to the difficult truths about how schools fail our students.

If we revisit purpose, intentionality, perception, persistence, interaction, and negotiation, how can we leverage student voice to support their agency? There is no silver bullet. Restructuring schools and reshaping instructional practices to support agency is complex and requires careful, dedicated, and critical examination. Much like these responses highlight, however, students are positioned all too often without a voice and without decisionmaking power. If we view agency solely as an individual trait or disposition, we neglect to capture how students are positioned in schools, as well as the structures and supports that aid or detract from their agency. Is it fair that the burden of student agency resides solely on the student? Think about the student who shared that if they go against what the teacher wants it would be "embarrassing," or the students' comment about going against what the teacher wants and then, in doing so, others perceiving them "as dumb" or one who causes "trouble."

Should supporting student agency be about students contesting the norms and practices in schools, or should schools support students in their efforts to be agentic? Should schools offer pathways and opportunities for students to be able to harness their agency? If we consider the role of smartness (Chapter 4) and the insights learned from these students' responses on agency, we see that students are positioned more often than not without agency. In the next chapter, we learn about what teachers have to say about student agency and the structures and supports they believe are necessary to support students in their agentic pursuits.

EXTENSION

Student agency requires listening and honoring students' voices. This requires listening to students and understanding their positions and perspectives. Select a few of the student quotes outlined in this chapter and write a reply to their responses. Reflect, after you have written your responses, on how you supported the following dimensions of agency:

- Dispositional: Intentionality and purpose. Do students feel as though they have purpose and support to pursue their ideas?
- Motivational: Perception and persistence. What are students' thoughts about the types of tasks they are doing?

- Positional: Interaction and negotiation. How are learning opportunities positioning students? Who are viewed as knowledgeable and smart and who has access to learning opportunities as a result? Are students able to share their lived experiences, languages, and cultural knowledge within the curriculum?

Did you encourage the student without putting the responsibility solely on the student? What are some recommendations for the teachers and schools of these students?

CHAPTER 6

How Teachers Implement and Talk About Agency

> Student agency is crucial for students because it gives them indepen-
> dence and voice. This is essential in establishing a classroom community
> because it gives them a sense of belonging and grants value to their
> diverse perspectives. This is also scaffolding them in being agents of
> change by taking part in civil discourse and setting forth the expecta-
> tions they will have as a citizen.
>
> —3rd-grade teacher, female

Teachers are essential in the construction of student agency. Much like
Johnston (2004) suggests, teachers help to create bridges to cultivate
student agency in classrooms through their dialogue and actions. For example, Ms. Kline, a 1st-grade teacher, teaching in the Pacific Northwest,
sat down to conduct a read-aloud on land forms to kick off her science
unit. Her students sat on the carpet and got ready to hear the informational text. Before starting, Ms. Kline asked students to share and pair
with one another and tell what they know about volcanoes. Ms. Kline
walked around the room and heard students excitedly share their stories of recent visits to the nearby National Park. She stopped her instruction and shared with students, "I hear so many experiences you've
had; how should we share these?" One student says, "We could tell
about our own stories." Another student says, "Ask our friends about
where they went." Yet another student says, "See if we could visit there
as a class." Ms. Kline says to students, "Okay, let's figure out what you
need to get started on developing your ideas" (Vaughn, 2020).

Classrooms where teachers structure opportunities to capitalize on
students' ideas, questions, and interests like this are central to supporting
and cultivating student agency in classrooms. Conversations with students and teachers like this where students' ideas, experiences, and ultimately their agency are included into the curriculum happen throughout

the day. Ms. Kline decided in the moment to support and expand on her students' interests, out-of-school experiences, and inquiries (Vaughn, 2019). In other words, she held an adaptive and flexible approach to her instruction so that her students could share the instructional floor with her. Her adaptive stance was critical in cultivating this opportunity for student agency. In this way, student agency in the context of schooling is negotiated and relies on individuals pursuing their interests and interacting with peers and their teacher. The teacher supports student agency and strengthens learning contexts where students' cultures, languages, and racial identities, and interests are in the foreground and where students and teachers are able to co-create learning contexts together.

Or consider another teacher, Ms. Simms, a special education teacher who teaches students from across grades in elementary and high school, who, after listening to her students' concerns about the social dynamics during recess, worked with her students to develop a knitting club at recess. To support her students, Ms. Simms asked her students about what type of club they were interested in and what they could do, and as a result they collectively decided on a knitting club. In the club, students practiced strategies for making friends, engaged in talking with others, and learned the skill of knitting. On the surface, this club could easily be viewed as another club in the school's extracurricular calendar. However, Ms. Simms listened to her students, engaged in dialogue with them, and learned that students were struggling to feel comfortable with talking with others at recess and took actions collectively to support her students. Teachers like Ms, Kline and Ms. Simms support students through their dialogue and actions, daily, hourly, and even minute by minute, to cultivate their students' agency.

Without understanding teachers' perspectives about student agency, we miss an important voice in conceptualizing agency beyond narrow views of agency (Cooren, 2010). Revisiting Bakhtin's (1981) notion of dialogism, and the role of multiple voices, this chapter provides a lens for examining teachers' perspectives about agency. Specifically, the focus is on the ways teachers' ideological views of agency are intertwined in complex learning communities. To understand the construction of student agency according to teachers, I asked teachers from across grade levels and regions to share their insights about student agency, what activities they believed supported student agency, and what schools could do to support their efforts to cultivate student agency.

Across teachers' responses about agency, they expressed a willingness for student agency and expressed targeted ideas for the ways in which schools should support students and their agency. In the following, themes are highlighted to express these ideas across interviews: agency as an opportunity for voice and choice, necessity of agency, and the flexibility and supports needed to cultivate agency. I then provide a critical discussion to mobilize insights about agency from Chapter 5 (students' perspectives on agency) and this chapter (teachers' perspectives on agency) with the aim of providing a contextualized view of agency from across these perspectives.

OPPORTUNITIES FOR VOICE AND CHOICE

Voice and agency are inherently linked as core dimensions of equitable schooling practices (Cammarota & Romero, 2011; Campano et al., 2013). Students use their voice to make decisions and follow their ideas and intentions. One compelling manifestation of voice and agency can be found in schools and in communities where students are invited to share their voice about topics and issues relevant and meaningful to their lives. For example, Gultom et al. (2019), in their work with adolescent and high school students from diverse racial, linguistic, and cultural backgrounds, explored issues of social justice and educational equity among marginalized youth and found that through research, students were able to critically examine the inequities in their communities and provide insight and a "community of resistance" (hooks, 1990, p. 388). Students provided a voice into their learning and community and were "social actors and experts on their own lives" (Cowie & Khoo, 2017, p. 234). In doing so, these actions provided opportunities for teachers to learn from their students and to enact culturally relevant pedagogy anchored in students' lives, cultures, and backgrounds (Cook-Sather, 2020).

Promising results were found in many of the teachers' responses about the role of student voice and choice in depictions of student agency. Teachers expressed that agency reflects student voice, choice, and decisionmaking—all of which they stated as essential in the learning process. For example, when asked to describe what student agency means in the context of schooling, teachers overwhelmingly described that agency reflected the need for students to share their voice and possess a role in the decisionmaking process. Illustrative examples from teachers are included to highlight these depictions of student agency.

"Student agency means that students have a choice in their learning and that their thoughts and opinions are heard."—5th-grade teacher, male

"Student agency is giving students ownership in their learning. It is making sure that their voice feels honored and that they care about their learning because they have been given choices. This is particularly important to me because I want to provide culturally responsive curriculum that meets the needs of my Native American students."
—1st-grade teacher, female

"Student agency gives students the opportunity to use their own voice when it comes to their learning and have options."—7th-grade teacher, female

"I believe that student agency means that students have a say in determining how they learn and, through guidance, what they learn."
—High school teacher, female

Teachers' responses emphasize the role of voice and choice in conceptualizations of student agency and the ways in which students should provide insight and direction into learning outcomes. Of interest is the parallel between students' perspectives about student agency as representing an avenue to share their voice and to make choices (as shared in Chapter 5) and teachers' perspectives on the necessity of student voice and choice in conceptualizing a view of student agency. In the following, teachers were further asked to share if and why they thought agency was something that was needed in schools.

NECESSITY OF AGENCY

Teachers expressed a deep connection to how student agency intersected with deeper learning and student achievement. Interestingly, teachers expressed the understanding that agency has the potential to develop higher student achievement and increased motivation and engagement. The following examples contextualize the ways in which the teachers expressed the role of agency in increasing student learning outcomes.

"I think it's absolutely crucial for students to have agency in the classroom. I believe that student agency leads to students who are more

engaged and motivated to learn, which leads to higher achievement."
—3rd-grade teacher, male

"Students who are given a voice in their learning are able to describe what they need to learn as well as what they want to learn. Students who have choices in their learning are, in my experience, happier and higher achieving than students who have everything they do directed by the teacher."—4th-grade teacher, female

"In my view, student agency boils down to students knowing themselves as learners and collaborators in their education. They see how they learn, the kinds of things or depth to which they want to learn, and how to show what they learn. They have a voice in their learning, thereby empowering them to direct themselves and others in how to get to the content that is offered to them."—8th-grade teacher, female

"Student agency means students discuss, explore, and make specific decisions about content or learning processes. Ideally everyone contributes to the conversation without judgment or fear of being judged, whether working in small groups or as a class. If there are clear guidelines for students to follow, they often take more risks in expressing their thoughts than without guidance."—High school teacher, female

As these responses suggest, teachers believed that student agency aligned with increased engagement, motivation, and learning. Across these ideas of student agency, teachers articulated the necessity of agency in schools. Such a finding positions agency as an important dimension of classroom practice. Scholars identify the role of student agency in supporting student learning outcomes. For example, Ivey and Johnston (2013) describe how engaged reading and agency in a middle school context was cultivated through the use of classroom structures and the young adult literature that students selected. Their research identifies the importance of providing choice and autonomy during instruction, specifically in the types of opportunities teachers provide in their planning of engaged reading opportunities. A sense of agency was found as students were able to discuss their ideas with one another and question each other. Brown (2020) said that to cultivate agency in mathematics learning contexts across schooling the view of the teacher as the "authoritative dispenser of disciplinary knowledge and skill" (p. 321) must be enacted differently. In contrast, students must be viewed as active learners, where they possess the knowledge and skill central to the learning task. Important to this is understanding how teachers structure tasks in their day-to-day practice in relation to student agency.

Interestingly, teachers shared examples from their classrooms about activities and lessons that they believed supported student agency. In the following, samples from across these responses are shared to highlight teachers' perspectives.

"Utilizing a culturally responsive curriculum must be part of developing student agency. It creates connections and allows students to share their heritage and draw upon their unique background knowledge. I have students help to create rubrics as well to support their ideas and align with developing their agency. Having students participate in the creation of a rubric helps them take ownership of their learning. It motivates them to do their best because they developed the criteria and know what success looks like. A writer's workshop model also aligns with developing my student's agency. I work with my students to publish books that are culturally responsive. It has been a very powerful way to develop their agency."—2nd-grade teacher, female

"In my class, I ask students to identify an issue that they care about to share with the class. I call it 'Sound Off!' This is a speaking and listening assignment, but it is also an opportunity for kids to find their voice and speak out. It is important on many levels. For one, students are able to share issues they care about, defining their opinions for themselves and revealing their thoughts to their classmates. These can be issues related to the school, our community, our country, or the world. This is a highlight of the week, as students present issues and share both sides of the issue. They state their own opinion, giving reasons for it. Then the class is invited to discuss the topic together. It is very empowering to students to speak their minds and to have peer feedback."—5th-grade teacher, female

"In math, I have been inviting students to reflect on their learning in regards to specific learning targets after summative evaluations. They have a menu of follow-up activities they can engage in to further their understanding of learning targets that continue to challenge them. It's tricky to find time to fit the 'second chance' learning activities and reassessments, but I am working on restructuring my math instruction time to address this."—4th-grade teacher, female

"One way I support student agency is to teach students to reflect on their learning, decide what they need to do to grow as a learner, set goals to meet the learning target, and reflect on where they are in relation to their goals. I do other things too, like I confer with each student to discuss [their] goals and learning path, ask students about what books they read based on their interests and reading abilities and also ask students what they want to work on during my 'genius hour'—project-based learning time. They get to choose a topic like an iMovie, an infographic, a slide show, or something else and demonstrate how they want to research it and present it to the class."—2nd-grade teacher, female

"I incorporate group work, collaborative projects, and independent work that offer students opportunities and choices to interpret, analyze, understand, create and apply their learning as some examples of activities that provide opportunities for students to practice student agency. If there are some solid/researched choices of how to work with material in digital learning, for example, students are left to ponder which avenue of expression they feel comfortable with or most enjoy using or are familiar with or want to strike out in a new medium of expression or play with a new tool. These choices offer students an exciting menu of choice and represent true diversity and respect for their varied ways of learning. When this respect and expectation of differen-tiation that we know exists among learners, students feel like they have control in how they can show up for learning."—High school teacher, male

"In movement classes students are given background instruction regarding several concepts of dance. Then they are placed in small groups to choreograph a dance using their own ideas based on the specific dance concepts. They contribute and discuss ideas, knowing that every person must contribute to the process, and no one person is allowed to 'veto' another's ideas. Students plan, practice, and perform their work for their class."—Middle school music/ dance teacher, female

"In my science class, we incorporate a practice called sharing thinking, where students work together to share what their thinking is as a group. We develop class norms where all students can be heard and work to develop trust in the classroom."—Middle school science teacher, female

"At the secondary level, students often have choice of what they read in terms of independent reading books. During research projects, students choose their topic of focus as well as their purpose for writing/ researching and the means by which they display that writing. For example, I recently did an informative writing unit in which students chose topics from high-interest categories; then they created a product of their choosing (PowerPoint, infographic, brochure, etc.)."—High school teacher, female

"When teachers intentionally integrate the necessary scaffolds and strategies for increasing self-regulation and reflection, students are provided with the opportunity to practice these skills, experience challenges and success, and increase their self-efficacy."—High school teacher, female

Across the responses, teachers expressed targeted practices they believed would support student agency. Teachers expressed opportunities for student choice and voice, flexible opportunities to display student learning, as well as flexible grouping structures and activities where students could share and revise their thinking based on new learning. As teachers expressed these ideas for students, I then asked what they needed to support student agency in their immediate classroom and school.

FLEXIBILITY AND SUPPORTS

When asked about what teachers needed to support student agency in their classrooms, they shared that they needed the flexibility and support to be viewed as professional decisionmakers with the ability to deviate from standardized curricula. In addition, many of the teachers emphasized the need of maintaining an open and positive outlook toward their students and their work as educators.

"Being able to diverge from strict adherence to 'the text book' is an important aspect. If I don't feel empowered to create systems in my classroom to give students choice, then it's not going to happen. Fortunately, my principal is supportive."—5th-grade teacher, female

"In order to support student agency in my classroom I needed an open mind. I needed to stop over explaining and directing and let kids figure things out. I had to get comfortable with productive struggle and realize that I'm actually hurting kids when I do things for them that they can do for themselves. I needed to stop saying things like, 'They aren't ready or they can't do this,' and instead trust them. They surprise me and amaze me every time, and for the ones who struggle, I offer scaffolds and support to help them be successful."—High school teacher, female

"I need the administration to support me financially and professionally so that I am able to offer choices in learning mediums along with opportunities to collaborate with teachers in the form of PLCs [professional learning communities]. I also need to include parent education so that parents are aware of how their student learns and what models best suit their child's learning needs."—Middle school teacher, female

"To support student agency in my classrooms I need the trust of my administration and colleagues first. Then I need to think through the processes I want students to experience and anticipate problems or roadblocks they might have. I front load instruction with background knowledge and clear expectations that focus students' attention on expressing appropriate ideas freely. I also emphasize that students always give their best effort. Voices speak/sing best in an environment where everyone understands the expectations and trusts that other students support their ideas."—ELL high school teacher, female

"More supports from my school about routinizing autonomous, asynchronous learning now that we are doing hybrid learning contexts with technology."—High school teacher, female

"I need a well-stocked library, and I need time for me and other adults and students to read and recommend/talk about books. The combined enthusiasm and communication about books gets reluctant readers engaged. I need a plan to help guide students through examples about ways to utilize agency and still cover the standards. For example, I would like to design assignments that give students agency over content but include them utilizing skills and strategies that I must teach."
—4th-grade teacher, male

"In order to support student agency, it is important to have an open mind, have strong relationships with students, good communication skills. It is also important to talk to other teachers about how they promote student agency in their class and find ways to transform that into one's own classroom."—3rd-grade teacher, female

"In order to support student agency in your classroom you need to be constantly building a culture where everyone present is respected, heard, honored and valued. You need to always have a vision of how best learning can occur and be willing to reflect on and allow the flexibility of your thinking to be influenced by student input. You need the space and resources to provide the variety of resources and time needed for all students."—Middle school teacher, female

"Clear expectations, consistency, and the willingness to remove supports."—High school teacher, female

"I think the most important thing that supports student agency in my classroom is to know students well. I think it is important for all students to be seen, heard, and valued. Once a student feels valued, then they are often willing to contribute to their learning and to the class in ways that lead to authentic learning, curiosity, advocating, and being genuine."—5th-grade teacher, female

What follows are teachers' depictions of agency as a necessary aspect of classroom practice. When asked if teachers feel that students should have agency and if they valued the idea of agency in schools, they responded in the following ways:

"I do believe that it's important for students to have agency because they need to have some control of how they want to learn."—High school teacher, female

"I think it's important for students to feel like they have a voice in the classroom. It's easy for people to feel passive, for us to sit back and let someone else 'drive the bus.' Learning is not like that. Learning is an active process, and if students aren't activated, very little learning can take place. Students need to understand that their choices make a difference. Sparking a sense of efficacy, a feeling that what you do makes a difference for yourself and those around you, is key."—5th-grade teacher, female

"Yes—I think students should be (and feel) empowered to solve problems in ways that make sense to them, speak up for themselves, address their needs, and have confidence to share their genuine self."—8th-grade teacher, female

"Students should have agency in the classroom. I believe that all people learn better when they have a say in what and how they learn. I personally find it motivating to learn new information in an organic fashion. . . .I have a question based on a need for information so I am motivated to pursue the answer with determination."—Learning specialist (various grades), female

As the teachers shared, students should have agency in the classroom to allow for more meaningful learning opportunities, engagement, and higher achievement. One teacher captured this overall sentiment and shared,

> "I think students should have agency in the classroom as much as possible, once they have the information they need to make informed decisions. They 'buy in' to learning processes, classroom organizational systems, and content more readily. In my experience, students who take part making choices in the learning process retain information better and take the initiative to peer tutor those who need help. Students thrive in a culture of structured routines that also allow the flexibility for small and large group work on projects and assignments."—5th-grade teacher, female

Teachers' responses emphasize the role of voice in their conceptualizations of student agency and the ways in which students should provide insight and direction into learning outcomes. Much like in Chapter 5, where students expressed that agency means the ability to share their voice and make choices, teachers shared that voice and choice were essential when describing student agency. Teachers' responses emphasize the importance of student voice in their depictions of student agency and the ways in which students must have a say in the direction of learning outcomes.

However, despite these affirming descriptions of agency as means of empowerment and a vehicle by which students' voices and decisions were central to the curriculum, interestingly, some of the teachers expressed some caution about agency as a tool. For example, one middle school teacher shared, "Student agency is the space that adults allow that encourages students to be curious, ask questions, seek answers, and take responsibility for their own learning. Some students rise to this opportunity independently; however, many students need to be taught directly and through examples of what student agency is and how to take advantage of it."

Such a response highlights how teachers and schools must possess critical and careful reflection of their views of agency. Viewing agency as something granted to students is antithetical to supporting student agency. Agency cannot be viewed as a tool that adults allow and one that may be granted to those individuals in classrooms, deemed readily able to receive it (think back to Mae and James in Chapter 4). Continually, scholars emphasize that structural inequality has led to contexts where schools rarely support students' agency, particularly students of color, students who are living in poverty, and students whose primary language is not English (Donnor & Shockley, 2010; Flores & Rosa, 2015). We see this inequity evidenced in the ways in which curricula is narrowed in subject areas. For example, in literacy instruction, a common subject area where students are routinely tested on their performance, students have few opportunities for agency, decisionmaking, and choice in their roles as readers and writers, or in math instruction, where historically teachers are viewed as the knowledgeable decisionmakers and where students are the passive recipients. This view of learning, where students lack a voice and decisionmaking power, is how schools are often structured. Moreover, recent educational reform efforts have exacerbated restrictive contexts for teachers, resulting in significantly narrowed learning experiences for students not conducive to fostering student agency (e.g., National Governors Association Center for Best Practices & Council of Chief State School Officers, 2010; U.S. Department of Education, 2009).

A view of agency as a tool granted to some and not others calls into careful reflection of how the hidden curriculum (Apple, 1975; Jackson, 1968) intersects with agentic opportunities for students, most importantly for students of color and those from nondominant backgrounds. The hidden curriculum "posits a network of assumptions that, when internalized by students, establishes the boundaries of legitimacy" (Apple, 1975, p. 99). From a critical stance, such an orientation of agency echoes the resulting outcomes implied by viewing smartness as a tool by which some students are granted access and others are not. Such a "sorting hat" implies that some students are capable of handling agency and others are not.

> The hidden curriculum deals with the tacit ways in which knowledge and behavior get constructed, outside the usual course materials and formally scheduled lessons. It is part of the bureaucratic and managerial "press" of the school—the combined forces by which students are induced to comply with the dominant ideologies and social practices related to authority, behavior and morality. (McLaren, 2008, p. 70)

Critical examination outlines that far too often students of color and those from marginalized backgrounds are not afforded opportunities like that of their White peers (Kohli et al., 2017). Agency is inextricably linked to smartness, identity, and the hidden curriculum that envelops learning communities, where smartness, identity development, and access to resources are intertwined with one's access to agency. Perspectives about agency as a tool to be granted to some students and not others requires critical examination of schoolwide practices for students of color and from nondominant backgrounds.

How can schools support an equitable view of agency? One particularly troubling response, when talking with an 8th-grader about opportunities for student voice and choice in his school, or potential opportunities for agency, occurred as he shared, "I never learned what agency means . . . a clear example of how our schools have failed us" (8th-grader, male).

There is no simple answer to these questions. However, a view of agency as a tool to be granted to some and not others underlies the structural inequality and institutional racism embedded in schools where some students have access to opportunities and others do not. As illustrated repeatedly in research (Au, 2007; Delpit, 2001), marginalized students and students from nondominant backgrounds are repeatedly left behind when it comes to advancing opportunities for agency, choice, and decisionmaking in schools. To counter this, schools, teachers, and researchers must critique and carefully reflect on learning opportunities to ensure equitable learning opportunities are in place. Many of these teachers' perspectives on agency and their important understandings about the ways in which they structure opportunities for agency are promising in moving toward more equitable practices conducive to supporting student agency.

EXTENSION

Consider the ideas presented in this chapter and what this might mean for you in your classroom or as a teacher alongside of these teachers.

1. What are some ways that you support student agency? Do you feel supported in your school/community to support your students' agency?
2. If so, what are the supports, and how could you explain these to another colleague at a different school who wants to develop a classroom/schoolwide culture focused on student agency?
3. Brainstorm ideas of what student agency means to you and the existing supports and structures you have in place to support your students. What else do you need to extend student agency in your school and broader community?

CHAPTER 7

Teaching for Student Agency

> The development of student agency includes creating mechanisms
> through which students are included in the meaningful process of
> analyzing teaching and learning such that their voices and perspectives
> inform classroom practices.
>
> —Cook-Sather (2020, p. 321)

A theory of learning that values learning as a social interaction rather than in the possession of an individual like a teacher, for example, is a discursive activity, socially negotiated and co-constructed in complex learning environments. In schooling, student agency is tightly connected to the structures, dialogue, and supports teachers organize and practice with their students in their classrooms. While I didn't know it at the time, when teaching Jackson that 1st year of teaching, all three of these elements of agency (dispositional, motivational, and positional) were present in my interaction with Jackson and the bush hog event referenced in the Introduction.

When Jackson asserted that he knew more about farm life than I did, I chose to go along with it, respecting his intentions to take the lead and share his knowledge of farm life. In the process, he reflected on what would be the best way to share his knowledge of farming, and he learned that in my classroom he was welcome to make that decision. In essence, in my classroom he and his peers were positioned as knowledgeable students who were welcome to co-create classroom activities and norms. In this example, there were specific structures (availability of materials and resources as well as opportunities to share student creations like his farm books), dialogue (questions about his interests and designs, and what farm life was), and supports (suggestions about how to research topics).

This is not to suggest that it's always so simple. There were plenty of times that I didn't get it right and missed opportunities as well. As a new teacher, I was lucky to have a student like Jackson. Realistically and for most teachers, most of the time, there are serious tensions involved in providing opportunities for students to harness their agency. In particular, teachers often struggle to decide how much control they need to reserve for themselves and how much autonomy they can realistically hand over to their students. There is a delicate balance of autonomy and control centered on classroom structures and norms of which teachers are keenly aware.

Recently, for example, I observed the class of a 2nd-grade teacher, Ms. Nenko, who invited her students to choose their own books, identify interesting themes, and then lead their small groups in discussing them. In theory, the activity promised to engage all three dimensions of student agency. In reality though, the students floundered, unsure how to get a book discussion started, so Ms. Nenko stepped in and took charge, saying, "I can see we need some help. Let me model for you how to start a discussion in your group."

At this point, the challenge for Ms. Nenko was to figure out precisely how much scaffolding her students would need in order to take over the book discussions for themselves. She could easily have canceled the activity, reasoning that 2nd-graders are just too young for that amount of autonomy. In this case, however, she decided to try again. This time she provided students with a set of open-ended question prompts they could use to get things started, and they proceeded to have lively discussions.

In other words, efforts to promote student agency always require a balancing act. Teachers never cede control entirely. They always have to be ready to provide necessary supports, structures, and guidance. More specifically, teachers should do the following:

1. Teachers should be alert to students' readiness to assert themselves, guide their own learning, and make their own choices. In classroom curriculum and decisionmaking activities, teachers should invite students into the curriculum to reveal their knowledge, skills, cultural experiences, and language proficiency that they may want to bring into the curriculum. In essence, the learning needs to be meaningful and relevant to students' lives, interests, and inquiries. The moment that Jackson made it clear that he knew more than I did about farm life, I was presented with a dilemma. I chose to let him run with his interests, but I could just as easily have decided to redirect him, on the grounds that he didn't seem ready to take control in that way and would be better off following directions. Every day, teachers face dozens, if not hundreds, of these kinds of split-second decisions. Noticing these opportunities is essential in classrooms where agency occurs.

2. Teachers should reflect on their own classroom structures, materials, and assignments to make sure they allow for students to assert agency. Student agency flourishes when school activities, materials, and structures afford students with some amount of freedom to (1) make significant decisions about their learning; (2) voice their opinions about issues that matter to them, (3) challenge what they're taught, especially if their background equips them with a competing perspective, and (4) reflect on their obstacles and barriers to problem-solve and find alternatives. If they're committed to helping students develop a strong sense of agency, then teachers must think carefully about the way they organize the classroom, the materials they make available, and the kinds of discussions they encourage. I worry that if they're not predisposed to look for opportunities to cultivate student agency, then their default choice will be to tell students to get back on task. Taking a reflective stance is essential in classrooms where agency is cultivated.

3. Teachers should err on the side of giving students too much choice and freedom. And if students aren't ready for it, then teachers should scale it back (rather than giving up on it entirely). Teaching for student agency requires taking risks and adopting an adaptive stance toward instruction. Adaptive teaching is individualistic and specific to students' linguistic, cultural, and instructional needs. As a result, adaptive teachers make decisions in the moment based on student inquiries, instructional needs, and their cultural and linguistic strengths (Vaughn, 2019). Without an adaptive approach to instruction where teachers modify what they are doing based on what their students are doing, opportunities for agency are stifled.

4. Teachers should be particularly aware of the dialogue and language they use to support students' agentic paths. In classrooms where students are supported to use their agency, teachers use targeted language and dialogue to support this. Freire (2005) emphasizes the role of an educational stance where teachers support an "I wonder" perspective in students rather than "I [must] do." Johnston (2004) similarly echoes this orientation through the explicit dialogue teachers use in their work with children. Teachers can use questions like

"What problems did you come across today" (p. 32) and "Which part about this are you unsure about?" (p. 34). Similarly, in my research with adaptive and flexible teachers, they use targeted language, asking students, "What do you know?" "I wonder why," and "Can you tell me more?" Central to supporting student agency is noticing how language can be used as a tool to support students' agentic pathways.

By providing educational contexts in which agency can be nurtured, educators create contexts where students are in charge of their learning and imagine alternative possibilities and pathways. Such rich learning spaces can provide generative contexts where students can problem-solve, imagine, and create new possibilities.

WHAT DOES AGENCY LOOK LIKE IN THE CLASSROOM?

To build on student agency and to support outlined dimensions of agency presented in earlier chapters (i.e., purpose, intention, persistence, perception, interaction, and negotiation), educators can think of the following steps to supporting and cultivating student agency. Figure 7.1 shows a recursive cycle that can be used to conceptualize how to weave students' intentions and purpose and ultimately guide them to persist, negotiate, and interact in order to accomplish and work toward their vision.

Figure 7.1. Cycle of Cultivating Student Agency

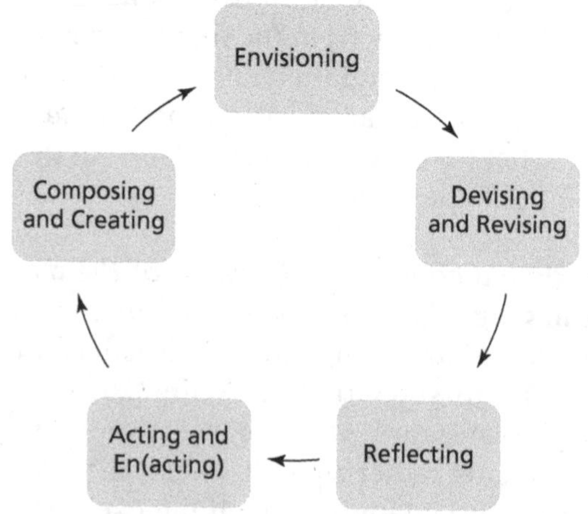

Envisioning

The role of visioning is an important component of teaching and developing a consciousness in educators to cultivate student agency. Duffy (2002) describes visioning as "a passionate commitment and mission" (p. 340). In this context, Duffy discusses the need for educators to possess a vision as they articulate what it is they wish to accomplish in their teaching. Others also echo the role and need for visioning as teachers connect their ideal image of classroom teaching to their actual classroom practice. Maxine Greene (1988) approaches such a call as developing a personal reality regarding teaching, developed in part through experiences, interests, and often based on moral convictions. That is, teachers with a vision have a "particular standpoint" and are "conscious, interested and committed" to that viewpoint (Greene, 1988, p. 26). Duffy (2002) further suggests that visioning links "the inner teacher and independent thinking" (p. 334). Similarly, Shulman and Shulman (2004) argue that teachers with a vision may be more likely to reflect on their practice, evaluating their instruction based on what their students need. Moreover, Hammerness (2001) articulates that a vision of what could be may also allow teachers to imagine other possibilities.

Teachers need visions inclusive of developing agentic students who are capable learners. These visions should then be tied to equitable instructional practices to ensure the gap between their vision and classroom practice is met. The following examples of teacher vision statements are likely to influence a sense of agency in students.

- My vision is to prepare students for life after school, whether that be college or entering the workforce-so to give them skills in the specific areas they need and to more generally know how to open up their ideas and figure things out. (Secondary technology teacher, female)
- My vision is that I think they need to learn and to understand. . . . Here's a concept; How does it apply to you in your real life? Can you use that or where will you use that in the future? (6th-grade teacher, male)
- My vision is that I want all my kids to be independent, compassionate, and productive members of society (Special education teacher, male)

- I would say that my goal is to develop well-rounded
  individuals . . . who are able to complete something,
  pull their experiences and knowledge and be able to
  be successful . . . to provide them with the skills that so
  they can use that for whatever they need in their future.
  (3rd-grade teacher, female)

Vision statements like this emphasize developing dispositional skills in students (productive, problem-solving, and independent) while emphasizing visions of fostering "a life beyond school" perspective so that students can transform knowledge and apply it to real life.

In addition to teachers, students also need to have the space in schools to develop their visions. In other words, we need to ask students what their vision is of themselves as a learner in school and what is it that they want to accomplish in a subject, month, year, and so on. Eliciting student visions of themselves helps teachers understand how they perceive their roles and identities in the classroom (see Figure 7.2). Teachers can use this information to explore how they can structure activities to build on these visions. Consider the following vision statement from one of the students with whom I've worked.

In this student's vision statement, she draws and shares, "My vision is to be a reader who reads all kinds off [of] books and learns from storys [stories]."Although this excerpt was developed when the student was asked "What is your vision of yourself as a reader and what do you want to accomplish this month in reading?" this same type of vision activity can be elicited from students across subject areas and about socioemotional learning goals. Intentionally asking students to reflect on their vision and to model to students how to deliver and act on their vision connects their purpose for what it is they are learning and doing.

Devising and Revising

As students conceptualize their vision, which connects their purpose and intentionality for the work it is that they want to accomplish, devising and revising is the essential next step in supporting and cultivating agency. Just as much as a teacher must plan their instructional activities, modeling to students and supporting students to plan specific tasks and goals to work toward their vision is integral in the process of developing agentic learning spaces. For example, in the provided vision statement, the teacher can then engage in a conversation

Figure 7.2. Vision Statement from a Student

My vision is to
be a reader who
reads all kinds off
books and learns from
the storys.

with the student and codevelop a plan toward "read[ing] all kinds off books." There are multiple ways to think about planning for this, from asking the student to create a list of questions about the topics they wish to pursue and modeling to the student how to use a variety of texts to find answers to these questions, to providing a guide for the student to track the types of books they are reading and reflecting and responding about what they learned from the texts. In this way, planning looks different depending on the task and the goals set forth by the student and teacher.

Consider another example of the ways in which devising and revising can occur through dialogue and discussion with students. A middle school student was interested in the women's suffrage movement and wanted to learn more about the topic. He expressed interest and then talked with his social studies teacher about possible ideas to demonstrate his knowledge about the topic. After discussing the topic and the student's vision and interest in the topic, the teacher and student codeveloped a learning plan to include a podcast about important women in the movement and to incorporate the podcast on the school's website so that the school and larger community could learn about the topic and the important figures. In this way, students *and* teachers are integral in the process of cultivating student agency. Without the necessary scaffolding and planning needed to support students' visions, opportunities to capitalize on student agency may be lost.

Reflecting

Just as teacher reflection is needed to help structure contexts conductive of agency, asking students about how and why they persist when experiencing challenges and reflecting about how they solved a problem or accomplished a goal invites them into the process of co-creating spaces where their voice is heard and honored. For example, reflection can occur during larger projects like the women's suffrage movement example, where the teacher asks the students content-oriented questions (e.g., What are you learning about the topic?), procedural questions (e.g., How are you compiling the information? and What do you need to make your podcast?), and questions about conceptual knowledge (e.g., What about this process is helping you think about yourself as a learner? What might you do differently next time, and why?). Moreover, reflective questions to support modeling to students about persisting can occur in the daily tasks we structure in subject areas. For example, when reading, asking students to tell how they figured out an unknown word or sharing their thinking during a hands-on math lesson are powerful ways to position students as knowledgeable and able to exert influence. Supporting student thinking and reflection like this is essential when learning about what students need and who students are, particularly as it comes to supporting their agency. Consider the following exchange with students in my research:

Michael, a 3rd-grader, during one observation after lunch seemed unhappy. His teacher, Ms. Milley, asked him, "Michael, what are you thinking?" Michael seemed to immediately switch facial expressions and shared his disappointment about the bullying at school he witnessed.

Ms. Milley asked, "Tell me more." Michael shared that he was thinking that the school could do some kind of anti-bullying project. Ms. Milley listened to his suggestion and shared, "What an important idea. What do you need to get started on your idea?"

Listening to Michael's ideas and picking up on his idea and suggestion was a powerful way Ms. Miley built on developing student agency. She engaged in reflective dialogue and switched back and forth from planning to reflective questioning to elicit just what Michael envisioned to work toward his ideas. Like this, teachers can use dialogue and help support students as they work toward developing their agency by asking questions and listening. Asking students to reflect and share their ideas and thoughts about what they create can be a powerful way to cultivate their agency.

Acting and (En)acting

As students envision, devise, and reflect on their purpose, intentions, and overall vision for what it is they want to accomplish, they enact the identity of someone capable of pursuing and negotiating their ideas. They act on their intentions and purpose to pursue their goals. As students are situated in complex, social environments and positioned (as seen in students' responses in Chapter 5) all too often as passive learners, this component within the recursive cycle of supporting student agency is critical when envisioning ways to cultivate student agency in schools. Teachers must adopt an adaptive stance, one where they fully embrace ways to co-construct learning outcomes and the instructional floor with students. Without teachers and schools supporting this dimension of the cycle, student agency can be stifled.

Composing and Creating

Throughout this process, students reflect, devise, and reflect and re-envision a variety of possible paths toward accomplishing their goals. They take action and engage in a process of composing and creating. Sometimes this is in a tangible manner (e.g., an artifact, a product) or could also be in dialogue or through their actions and participation. It is during this phase in the cycle where students choose and make decisions about the ways in which they want to exert their vision, purpose, intentions and in a broader sense—their agency. This cycle can be supported by specific instructional practices.

INSTRUCTIONAL PRACTICES

In my research with teachers and students and the research of others, there are some valuable instructional practices that can be structured in classrooms to support the cycle outlined, and in doing so ultimately support student agency. The following are practices that can be used to share the instructional floor with students and invite students into the curriculum.

Voicing

Activities where students can share their voices are essential when cultivating student agency. Such practices include inviting students to lead "Bless This Book" (Marinak & Gambrell, 2016). In this practice, typically teachers select a book and, in essence, bless the book, thereby encouraging students to read the book. One way to adapt this practice to engage students and to provide an experience where students can take a more active role is to invite students to lead the Bless This Book activities in class and share their recommendations with others (Fisher & Frey, 2018). Students can choose a book and encourage others to read the book based on their recommendation. In this way, students have a different role in the process: They are no longer passive participants but take on the role of leader as they share their own personal interests in books.

The benefits of literature circles have also been well documented in the literature to increase student participation and to encourage dialogue about students' connections and interests in books (Daniels, 2002; Raphael et al., 2001). Dialogical contexts like this encourage students to challenge their ideas, ask other questions, and develop the ability in students to share their perspectives.

Project-Based Learning

Project-based learning (PBL) is an instructional practice where students engage in complex, real-world tasks that result in a product (Barron & Darling-Hammond, 2008). These inquiry projects are centered on a product and give students hands-on opportunities to work with others and materials and present their work. Projects are driven by student questions and inquiry, and students are supported as they work to perform their own investigations, develop answers, and voice their opinions throughout the learning (Merritt et al., 2017; Tal et al., 2006). Such learning opportunities are student driven, and teachers facilitate students' interests.

In a 4th-grade classroom in the Pacific Northwest, given students' interest on the local steelhead trout and fishery in the community, Ms. Jaye engaged students in a PBL unit to learn about other environmental issues surrounding trout. Students often shared about their expeditions to the nearby river with their families to fish for trout. Annually, the class took a trip to visit the local dam where there was a hatchery. In the newspaper, there were many different letters to the editor about whether the local dam should be supporting the hatchery or letting the salmon survive on their own. This was a heated debate for many households, according to Ms. Jaye, who shared that at least half of her students either fished in the river or had relatives who worked in the hatchery.

Students were working on creating an informational brochure for the community about the opposing sides and perspectives. During this unit, Ms. Jaye facilitated discussions and asked students several questions to elicit their ideas and the details they learned. Oftentimes when I observed during this unit, I could hear Ms. Jaye say, "I don't know; let's find out!" (Vaughn & Parsons, 2013).

Multimodal Designing

Multimodal workshops and multimodal representations (Jiang et al., 2020; Kuby & Vaughn, 2015) provide spaces where students can play around with materials to include productions and create multimodal artifacts about their inquiries and interests. Through these multimodal encounters, students can harness their agency and become teachers, producers, and visionaries. Opening spaces like this in the curriculum can serve as opportunities whereby students can harness a sense of agency—acting on their thoughts, talk, multiple modes, materials, and ideas to produce artifacts. In research of multimodal workshop practices, I noticed moments of agency not only in what students produced but also in the process of creating—choices about materials, topics, genres, and which peers to collaborate with on projects.

Remote learning can support opportunities for student agency where students are able to engage more freely in exploration and teachers can structure more opportunities for student choice. Consider a teacher with whom I work. She is learning how to navigate a new online learning platform to support units of study that are interesting to her students.

First, before she began her planning, she sent a questionnaire to students asking what topics in U.S. history were interesting to them and what they want to learn and why. By first asking students what topics and areas they'd like to pursue, the teacher was then able to break students into smaller, collaborative research groups in which she set up tasks and open-ended learning assignments for students to complete. For example, students were able to choose from a variety of assignments to perform individually and collectively within the group. One group chose the rights of immigrants past and present. Students could choose to write their own historical fiction essay where they inserted themselves into a time in the United States where immigrants fled to the nation, conduct a mock interview with one another where they could ask each other important questions about the rights of immigrants, or create their own multimodal presentation displaying their knowledge. In this way, as remote learning becomes more a part of the fabric of how teachers and students do school, such opportunities are structured to offer students compelling avenues to pursue their interests and passions.

Student agency flourishes when teachers and students articulate visions for what it is they want to accomplish as well as connect their visions to intentions and beliefs. Specific instructional practices and structures can afford students with some opportunities to harness agency. Agency allows for students to (1) make significant decisions about their learning; (2) voice their ideas, (3) challenge perspectives, and (4) problem-solve, thereby creating alternative solutions. Teachers must be adaptive in their approach and must think carefully about the way they organize the classroom, the materials they make available, and the kinds of discussions they encourage as they work toward developing agentic students.

EXTENSION

Student agency is a complex process involving careful thought and reflection about the types of structures and supports in schools. Reflect on the following questions:

- What is your vision for yourself as a teacher? Why?
- What is your vision for students? Why?
- What is your vision for school/ community? Why?
- What instructional practices, outlined in this chapter, are most meaningful to you? Why?
- What are additional strategies and supports you can structure to cultivate student agency in your classroom and school community?

CHAPTER 8

Cultivating a Culture of Agency

Thus, by choosing and shaping their environments, people can have a hand in what they become.

–Bandura (2001, p. 11)

How do we create a culture of agency in schools to expand students' agentic lives? What would schools and classrooms look like for students, teachers, and communities? When we think about student agency in today's schools, we may struggle to conceptualize how the two can fit together. Recent educational reform efforts (e.g., National Governors Association Center for Best Practices & Council of Chief State School Officers, 2010; No Child Left Behind Act (2002); U.S. Department of Education, 2009) have resulted in learning contexts not focused on fostering student agency.

It is important to understand that in addition to *experiencing* the primary context of schooling, students also *negotiate and co-construct* their identities through *improvisations* (a process of "making worlds" (Holland et al., 2001). Bakhtin's (1986) notion of "self-authoring," whereby identities and agency are continually co-constructed in a process of remaking and reshaping, shows that through this process students negotiate their sense of who they are in schools. In effect, their agency is tightly connected to their identity; thus, identity, skill, and agency are therefore codeveloped as they interpret and improvise in school.

Undoubtedly, as Johnston (2004) states, "In schools, it is our job to help expand the possible agentive narrative lines available for children to pick up" (p. 40). What could happen in schools if we cultivated a culture of agency? How can schools possibly do this? Given the current racial tensions in the nation that have heightened the structural inequalities manifested in schools, where students of color, students who are living in poverty, and students from homes where English is not the primary language (Flores & Rosa, 2015) have been denied agency, the time to examine how agency can become part of schools' core beliefs and behaviors is vital.

The focus of this chapter is looking at how to shift and change structures within schools to support student agency. School culture is strengthened by people, interactions, and connections and developing core beliefs and behaviors (Green, 2017). Thus, in the following, drawn from understandings from educational leadership, participatory action research with teachers and students, and the theoretical framework outlined in this book, developing a culture of agency is outlined in three areas, the classroom teacher, the student, and the principal, centered on core beliefs and behaviors and interactions and connections.

THE CLASSROOM TEACHER

There is no quick fix to creating student agency; however, what I have stressed in this book is that there are underlying principles at work when working to foster student agency. Cultivating student agency is about supporting students so that their identities in practice are agentic and there is a deep focus on the role of reflection and questioning. As a result, questioning and reflecting on how students' intentionality and purpose can be embedded into daily structures, tasks, units, and leadership opportunities in the school is essential.

Asking ourselves questions about instructional practices; our beliefs about students, teaching, and schools; and how to support students' ideas and interests is essential. Careful reflection is needed to understand the tasks we structure and what students think about these tasks. It is essential to critically examine how students are positioned and the interactions and negotiations that we, as teachers, use to support and encourage students. We also must question what opportunities work for whom, when, and under what circumstances. Cultivating a culture of agency is about inviting and honoring students in a substantial and authentic manner—not as an add-on or something granted to some and not others. In order to develop a culture of agency, teachers must begin with reflective practice to understand their role in supporting students' dispositions and motivations and how their students are positioned in schools and in their classrooms.

For example, consider the exchange for student agency: During a discussion on the immigration policies in the United States in 2018, Mr. Vincent, an 8th-grade teacher, invited students to read firsthand accounts from parents separated from their children at the U.S. border. Mr. Vincent noticed how students were visibly upset, and rather than continuing with the social studies lesson, he invited his students to share what might be meaningful next steps. Students offered to write letters to the president, share their opinions, and use primary documents to support their positions to counter current policies. Another group of students decided to research local refugee groups to learn about volunteering opportunities. Some students preferred to respond in their notebook, others turned to a partner and talked about what they thought, while others raised their hand and asked questions. Mr. Vincent responded to his students in the moment, and in doing so strengthened his students' sense of agency.

Like this example suggests, adaptive and responsive teaching are critical when supporting opportunities for student agency. Boyd et al. (2020) emphasized the role of responsive teaching and how such teaching is anchored within student contributions. This responsiveness provides a bridge to meet students' interests, concerns, and the specific instructional situation at hand and serves as a means to cultivate student agency. Teachers like Mr. Vincent and others discussed in the book, who cultivate student agency in their classroom, possess characteristics evident in ways they support student agency. These teachers do the following:

- Honor and respect students' knowledge, linguistic abilities, racial identities, and home cultures
- Invite students' visions, ideas, and beliefs into all areas of learning
- Adopt a flexible and adaptive stance to teaching
- Engage in reflective practice, asking what practices are working, for whom, and under what circumstances

For the classroom teacher, cultivating a culture of agency begins with a focus on developing a vision for teaching that represents honoring and respecting students, inviting students' visions and ideas into the classroom, and adopting a flexible and adaptive approach to teaching. In addition, cultivating a culture of agency also relies on understanding how to mobilize teachers' individual and collective agency in their work. Teachers are what Cochran-Smith (2005) terms as the lynchpins in educational reform.

Teachers are the advocates of student agency. An advocate has what Sergiovanni (2001) states is that specialized knowledge of schools, the inner workings and uses, what Cochran-Smith and Lytle (2009) state their "social position to assist with the flow of information and to create opportunities for resources to accrue in support of a particular set of values or group of people" (p. 270). Through collective action research, a process by which teachers engage in reflective research together, they can "make observations that resemble one another that, when conceptualized together, begin to have explanatory power and general relevance" (Campano, 2007, p. 115).

THE STUDENT

As I was preparing to write this book, I reflected on my own role as a student, teacher, and researcher, and I am still taken aback after talking with two students about their experiences with agency in school:

> "I never learned what agency means . . . a clear example of how our schools have failed us."—8th-grader, male

> "I would like the choice of skipping the reward parties to read in the library, but other than that I'm fine with school the way it is. For me, agency means embarrassing myself or maybe annoying the teacher . . . and I don't really want to do that."—7th-grader, female

These students' responses are what no teacher or administrator wants to hear about their school or classroom. Yet, the idea that some students feel that acting with agency doesn't exist or would embarrass themselves or annoy the teacher is haunting and a testament to the importance of reshaping school culture toward student agency. Yes, students have a vital role in developing their agency. However, they are positioned in schools far too often as powerless. Student agency quite often has been targeted as something a student should harness and direct on their own behalf, viewing agency solely as an individual's responsibility. This view simply doesn't consider the collective bodies at work and the sophisticated hierarchies of power that exist in schools.

Student agency is linked to a complex process involving individuals, systems, experiences, and histories. Agency is "both individual and social. It is demonstrated through actions[across these dimensions]. Agency is flexible. Agency is embedded in past, present, and future actions" (Massey & Wall, 2020, p. 172). Thus, although this section is about recommendations for the student, these suggestions do not exist in a vacuum but between teachers, administrators, and students. The following recommendations come from across classrooms, where students enacted their agency. These common elements were found in ways to support students in their agentic efforts. In these classrooms, students do the following:

- Develop a vision for what it is they want to accomplish in a subject, school, etc.
- Reflect on their thinking and actions
- Engage in collaborative and individual work to support their ideas
- Utilize a variety of materials and modes to share and display their learning

In addition, scholars highlight the extent to which agency is cultivated in students through participatory research.

Youth participatory research provides a pathway for students to share their voices and provides a window whereby students can empower themselves and take an active stance toward what it is they are learning and doing in the world. In this way, students can provide insight and direction into the curriculum and this "co-construction of curriculum provides a context for students to change their relationships to their schools and communities to affect broader social, cultural, and political milieu" (Cochran-Smith & Lytle, 2009, p. 14).

THE PRINCIPAL

In order to develop a core belief of agency, administrators must interrogate their current school climate and the extent to which agency exists or is absent in their schoolwide leadership approach. Principals must reflect on how teachers and students are positioned in the school—from curricular decisions to routines and procedures, to school climate.

In my work with teachers, I am continually in awe of what they do—from constructing lessons to meeting students' interests, to analyzing data, to navigating classroom structures and state standards, to meeting the social emotional needs of their students. With incredible tenacity, grace, knowledge, and compassion, everyday teachers meet these demands in spite of the realities of a failing educational system with diminishing pay and supports. I am amazed by teachers and the work they do daily to support and meet students' needs. That is why I am so astonished by the lack of agency they experience while accomplishing these several daunting tasks (and more) in the matter of a school day. For example, consider a recent conversation with a teacher with whom I routinely work:

> *Margaret:* "Are you going to have students select their own books to read today?"
> *Teacher:* "No, we have to have students read from the curricular set."
> *Margaret:* "Why?"
> *Teacher:* "They told us we had to."

In this exchange, the teacher felt no agency about the types of books her students could read in her classroom (Vaughn, Scales et al., 2019). Although this conversation was close to 3 years ago, this conversation has long stayed with me. This teacher, a well-seasoned teacher, pursuing a master's degree in educational leadership, felt little to no agency. How is this possible, given that teachers like her face, meet, and master increasingly challenging demands and yet they feel little to no agency? Building a culture of student agency begins with developing a culture of agency for all—from students but also from teachers, staff, and parents. Based on research on effective school leadership, to cultivate student agency, principals must do the following:

- Provide shared decisionmaking and leadership
- Cultivate teacher agency through involvement in professional learning opportunities
- Honor and respect students' identities, home lives and background and visions for learning by inviting parents, family members, and community members into shared decisionmaking processes
- Facilitate practices supportive of student agency (see Chapter 7 for ideas)

Working toward student agency is complex and takes into account students' individual racial identities, backgrounds, languages, cultures, and instructional strengths. Recognizing these elements and understanding how teachers, parents, and family members are critical partners in developing agency is paramount. Figure 8.1 shows the steps for creating a shared vision of agency with teachers, students, and parents.

Figure 8.1. Steps to Cultivating a Culture of Agency

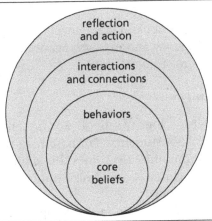

DEVELOPING CORE BELIEFS

In order to develop a culture of agency, teachers and administrators must interrogate their current school climate and the extent to which agency exists or is absent in their school. In doing so, they can identify core beliefs in their school and areas they need to address to focus on agency. Building a schoolwide culture of student agency begins with developing a culture of agency for all. Reflecting on current school core beliefs as they pertain to developing student agency can allow for meaningful conversations to take place. In doing so, administrators and teachers must critically examine the shared decisionmaking that does (or does not) take place in their schools. If teachers lack agency in their work as professionals, it is hard for them to imagine supporting agency in their classroom. Establishing a belief that agency is essential, an important part of the school and involves all individuals in the school, is essential. Asking the following questions can help:

For teachers

- What is my vision for teaching? For myself as a teacher? For students? For parents/guardians? And my school community? How does this align with supporting my agency as a teacher and my students' agency?
- What practices do I engage in that support my students' agency? What are the resources needed to accomplish this?

How will I know my students possess agency once I'm engaged in the practice?

- What does my school and grade level currently do to support my students' agency and my own agency as a teacher? What could be done to strengthen this?

For administrators

- What is my vision for my school? For myself as an administrator? For students? For parents/guardians? For my school community? How does this align with supporting my individual agency as an administrator and my students' and teachers' agency?
- What practices do I engage in that support students' and teachers' agency? (Be specific.) What are the resources needed to accomplish this? How will I know my students and teachers possess agency?
- What does my school and grade level currently do to support my students' agency and my own agency as an administrator? What could be done to strengthen this?

ENACTING BEHAVIORS

After reflecting and inventorying current core beliefs and behaviors, teachers and principals should then answer the questions in Table 8.1.

Table 8.1. How We Can Support Agency?

For teachers/administrators		
What does agency mean for me as a teacher/administrator?	What practices do I engage in to facilitate agency as a teacher/administrator?	What resources do I need to enhance my agency?
What does agency mean for my students?	What practices do I help structure to facilitate student agency?	What supports do I need to support my students' agency?
For students		
What does agency mean to me, and how can I build on this in my school/class?	What help do I need to build on my agency?	What can I do to use this in other subject areas?

Using this information, an action plan can be developed to support these areas. For example, conducting a read-aloud with younger students about what agency is, why it can help, and how to use it in learning and other settings can be shared. Engaging students in dialogue about agency and reflecting on activities that may enhance agency is essential. For example, Sharma (2008) found that 8th grade science students enacted their agency by engaging in science discourse when it resonated with their lives. In this way, reflecting on what instructional practices work (and don't work) can provide insight into ways to structure student agency.

INTERACTIONS AND CONNECTIONS

In many schools where there is a positive school culture and climate, students and teachers have a common vision of respect and of sharing the work to support all. Building interactions and connections as it pertains to cultivating a culture of agency can look different in schools— from having teachers lead professional development workshops in their schools and in the district to students conducting presentations for other grades or within the community, to developing schoolwide practices where students are engaged in positive interactions with one another. Maintaining interactions and connections aimed at fostering agency relies on engaging in reflective practice to ensure that all individuals are included and represented.

REFLECTION AND ACTION

Finally, teachers, principals, and students must engage in critical reflection. Asking about their participation supports the core beliefs and behaviors identified as important to agency for the group. The cycle of reflection to action continues throughout as in a checks and balance system to ensure practices support agentic opportunities.

In order to create a culture of agency in schools to expand students' agentic lives, schools must consider and question their current practices and beliefs. Developing a shared vision of what agency means at the school level, classroom level, and individual level (e.g., teacher, student, administrator) can help to provide a conceptual roadmap for schools in their efforts to develop a schoolwide culture of agency. Engaging in reflective practice and examining actions conducted in the school toward agentic practices and opportunities can provide insight and future direction into what steps can be taken to ensure equitable and agentic practices for all.

EXTENSION

Using the ideas presented in this chapter, develop an action plan for how to take steps toward these actions. Revisit your personal vision, invite students to create their own vision, and then work with colleagues in the school to support and develop a vision for supporting student agency. Developing a vision for cultivating student agency is a multifaceted process involving a variety of stakeholders. We can begin conversations with students by asking students to share what is working and what is not. Invite parents/guardians and community members to engage in these collaborative conversations.

CHAPTER 9

A Look to the Future

There is always possibility. And this is where the space opens for the pursuit of freedom.

–Greene (1988 p. 128)

When you see equitable learning spaces, what exactly do you see? How are individuals positioned? Whose voice gets heard and why? What materials and resources are available for free access? Ultimately, what are students doing? Continually, we know that in effective class-rooms where students are motivated to learn, teachers are supportive of their learning interests, cultures, histories, and inquiries (Mendoza et al., 2018; Zaccor, 2018). Moreover, we know from the literature on teacher practice that effective teachers lead students toward in-dependent decisionmaking and toward opportunities to express their agency (Pressley et al., 2001). Teachers and schools are instrumental in developing flexible spaces where students' voices and opinions are heard (Barton & Tan, 2010).

Agency is the ability of individual students to influence and to create opportunities in the learning context through intentions, decisions, and action. Throughout the chapters in this book, agency has been conceptualized to provide a portrait of what it means for students, teachers, and schools. Each chapter aims to understand the dimensions involved in cultivating agentic spaces in schools. As the nation faces political uncertainty and heightened racial inequities and injustice, the time for conversations about student agency are vital. It is my hope that the chapters provide a critical discussion on the nature of agency across contexts with an eye toward creating more equitable spaces in our nation's schools.

Where can we go from here in our understandings of student agency? A few understandings are essential before exploring this question: (1) Agency is a situational and collective and collabora-tive process; (2) student agency connects students' backgrounds, languages, stories, and identities in practice; and (3) student agency is interdependent and reconstructed in complex learning environments. In that, agency can be viewed as a tool that can be used to structure, restructure, and shape learning experiences for students in all too often restrictive school spaces, which Dyson (2020) emphasizes limits children in agentic ways. Agency is a sociocultural mediating tool that "youth and families [can] discern, within educational contexts, issues of power and inequity in order to act in a manner that enhances greater individual and community self-determination" (Campano et al., 2020, p. 224).

In writing this concluding chapter, I, like many others, have been debilitated by recent current events. Our nation has seen the consistent violence toward Blacks that compels a careful critique of how schools reinforce structural inequities for marginalized populations. Understanding and teaching for agency is needed now more than ever. Schools have the potential to reshape these narratives. Indeed, "Classrooms are not apolitical spaces but, rather, are sites of struggles and resistance over the potential life trajectories of students" (Hatt & Urrieta, 2020, p. 210). In keeping with what Giroux and Simon (1989) detail about pedagogy,

> Pedagogy refers to a deliberate attempt to influence how and what knowledge and identities are produced within and among particular sets of social relations. It can be understood as a practice through which people are incited to acquire a particular "moral character." As both a political and practical activity, it attempts to influence the occurrence and qualities of experiences. When one practices pedagogy, one acts with the intent of creating experiences that will organize and disorganize a variety of ways. . . . Pedagogy is a concept which draws attention to the processes through which knowledge is produced. (p. 12)

In this power of pedagogy, teachers and administrators must ask the questions, "What opportunities do I want my students to have for self-authorship and self-making (i.e., agency) in my classroom [and school]?" (Hatt & Urrieta, 2020, p. 212). This generative discussion in viewing agency from these positions helps to uncover how agency is "[a] contextually enacted way of being in the world" (van Lier, 2008, p. 3). In relation to schooling, the individual and collective are necessary, and neither can exist without the other in relation to one's agency. These two—the individual and the collective—work in tandem, as tightly connecting agency in schools.

Although such positions offer a compelling view of agency and the importance of student agency when it comes to student learning, I was once again reminded of why our collective work on student agency is needed as a principal with whom I work in my research asked, "But, does agency *really* matter?" (Vaughn, 2020, p. 239). I would argue that supporting student agency matters more than ever. We must as a community push back against such narrow views of what has mattered most in schools: student outcomes on standardized achievement. Undoubtedly, student outcomes do matter, but so does supporting student agency. Given the social inequities in schools and the polarizing racial discourse and violence toward marginalized populations in the United States, attention to student agency is not only needed but needed now more now than ever.

WHERE TO FROM HERE?

In sum, chapters in this book demonstrate that student agency is a navigational tool representing students' individual dispositions and motivations but situated in complex social spaces. Given that student agency is a distant goal for many schools, in this section, I provide implications for students, teachers, teacher-educators, administrators, and policymakers.

Students

Continue to recognize that your ideas, voice, and actions are important. You matter.

Teachers

Teachers are the gatekeepers in many ways as to whether students will have agency during learning situations. What might teachers do to support student agency? Adopting a flexible, adaptive, and reflective stance is of the utmost importance. Teachers must be willing to share the instructional floor with their students and support students as co-creators during learning opportunities. Adaptability is that type of teaching where teachers listen to their students' interests, queries, and experiences and co-construct learning opportunities alongside their students (Vaughn, 2019).

Adopting a reflective stance means that teachers must critically examine their practices to see how they can support the dimensions of agency presented in this book (i.e., dispositional, motivational, and positional). Teachers must carefully reflect on their vision, review their students' visions, and engage in dialogue with their students about their practice. In that, teachers must be willing to interrogate their practice and ask in what ways opportunities are structured for agency, for whom, and for what purposes. Much like Moses et al. (2020), teachers must be willing to critically unpack their beliefs about their instruction, student learning, and autonomy in their efforts to structure opportunities in their classrooms that can position students as agentic. Similarly, teachers need to learn of instructional practices that may facilitate agentic opportunities. For example, Brown (2020) emphasizes collective argumentation, and Cavagnetto et al. (2020) emphasize the role of authorship as a means to structure classroom instructional activities conducive to agency. Although there is no "silver bullet" to agency in the classroom, engaging in reflective practice to explore what works, for whom, and under what circumstances can help to illuminate pathways to student agency.

Learning of these instructional practices and reflecting on one's practice is essential. Supporting teacher agency may be an important link to student agency (Dyson, 2020; Robertson et al., 2020). Engaging in action research may be an important tool for teachers in these efforts. Action research "empower[s] teachers to examine their own beliefs, explore their own understandings of practice, foster critical reflection, and develop decision making capabilities that would enhance their teaching and help them assume control over their respective situation" (Ginns et al., 2001, p. 129). Using their research of their practice, teachers can work within schools and districts and inform how policy can be shifted to encourage more equitable practices conducive to supporting student agency.

Teacher-Educators and Professional Developers

Because teacher-educators and professional developers are in the position to support teachers in their professional journey, engaging in conversations about the role of student agency in structuring learning opportunities is essential. Take, for example, a recent concern in my department about our teacher education program. Teacher candidates want a classroom management course and schools encourage teacher education departments to teach classroom management to teacher candidates. Although I don't disagree, these conversations in our department almost always end in practices and approaches aimed at viewing learning where student agency is never discussed. Rather, conversations center on how teachers can control their students—tasks and opportunities for student choice and agency are never part of the equation.

It is critical to engage teacher candidates in conversations about what student agency is (and what it isn't) so that they can work against the apprenticeship of observation (Lortie, 1975), a phenomenon where beginning teachers will more than likely teach in similar ways they were taught. There are a variety of ways to engage in such conversations, such as using autoethnographic practices and counternarratives (Beucher et al., 2019; Vaughn & Kuby, 2019), where understandings about equitable learning practices in schooling, lived histories, and the role of agency can be critically and carefully unpacked. Massey and Wall (2020) suggest fostering an agentic mindset in teacher candidates, understanding the role of agency, and critically analyzing power structures and practices that may cultivate agency in students. Cochran-Smith (2020) highlights the important role of teacher-educators in their ways of working with teacher candidates to help shape views of teaching that counter the inequities we far too often see in schools.

For professional developers, professional learning spaces can be structured to support teacher professionalism. The role of professional development cannot be undervalued in looking to the future, in that developing sustained, professional development focused on student agency is essential (Bates & Morgan, 2018; Hargreaves, 2019).

Administrators and Policymakers

Student agency matters. Expanding our views in the field on what works in our schools is vital. Understanding the important role of student agency in relation to student learning is the next logical step. Listening to teachers' efforts about their decisionmaking processes when it comes to supporting student agency can augment supports for student agency. Reexamining the ways in which pay-for-performance benchmarks are reduced to student learning outcomes is reductionist. How can these benchmarks include more authentic measures? An example might be including action research or a whitepaper written by a group of teachers about their shift to supporting student agency.

Supporting teachers in their efforts to be flexible and adaptive is warranted and understanding that student agency is not an add-on are the logical next steps toward advancing student agency in schools. As a community, teachers, teacher-educators, administrators, and policymakers must work across paradigms and platforms to move agency into schoolwide practices.

Scholars and Researchers

Interestingly, the relationship between student agency, learning outcomes, or effective teaching is not well documented in the literature. Promising work has begun, however. Veiga et al. (2015) examined adolescents' agency; Ferguson et al. (2015) measured student agency with middle and high school students; and finally Vaughn, Premo et al. (2020) developed a survey to use with elementary students in their understandings of agency in literacy. However, more research needs to be conducted that explores the relationship of student agency to outcomes as well as other characteristics of teaching. More research needs to be done to highlight students' voices about their agency.

CONCLUSION

Student agency is essential in today's schools. It matters more now than ever. We must, as a community, advocate for student agency across dimensions in schools, teacher education, in service, and in policy and research. This book addresses the inner dimensions of student agency using classroom vignettes and stories. The aim is to provide a portrait of agency in schools—what it is and why it is needed. When students act on their sense of agency, they take action and initiate the direction of the instructional situation. Opportunities to support and to promote student agency can be easily missed. The goal of this book was not to place judgment on classroom teachers, but to illuminate opportunities during instruction as a way to build on student contributions and ultimately support student agency. Although many educators across the nation face enormous challenges and pressures to adhere to districtwide mandates to improve student performance on standardized assessments, we must continue to strive for developing students' agency. I invite you to reflect on agency as a navigational and advocacy tool so that practices in schools support all learners. Our students deserve to have agency.

References

Abodeeb-Gentile, T., & Zawilinski, L. (2013). Reader identity and the Common Core: Agency and identity in leveled reading. *Language and Literacy Spectrum, 23*, 34–45.

Ainley, M. (2006). Connecting with learning: Motivation, affect and cognition in interest processes. *Educational Psychology Review, 18*(4), 391–405.

Alvermann, D. E. (2001). Effective literacy instruction for adolescents. *Journal of Literacy Research, 34*(2), 189–208. https://doi.org/10.1207%2Fs15548430jlr3402_4

Apple, M. (1975). Scientific interests and the nature of educational institutions. In W. Pinar (Ed.), *Curriculum theorizing* (pp. 120–130). McCutchan.

Archer, M. (2000). *Being human: The problem of agency.* Cambridge University Press.

Archer, M. (2003). *Structure, agency, and the internal conversation.* Cambridge University Press.

Au, W. (2007). High-stakes testing and curricular control: A qualitative metasynthesis. *Educational Researcher, 36*(5), 258–267.

Bakhtin, M. M. (1981). *The dialogic imagination: Four essays by M. M. Bakhtin.* University of Texas Press.

Bakhtin, M. M. (1986). *Speech genres and other late essays* (V. W. McGee, Trans.). University of Texas Press.

Ball, C., Huang, K. T., Cotten, S. R., Rikard, R. V., & Coleman, L. O. (2016). Invaluable values: An expectancy-value theory analysis of youths' academic motivations and intentions. *Information, Communication & Society, 19*(5), 618–638.

Bandura, A. (1986). From thought to action: Mechanisms of personal agency. *New Zealand Journal of Psychology, 15*, 1–17.

Bandura, A. (1993). Perceived self-efficacy in cognitive development and functioning. *Educational Psychologist, 28*(2), 117–148.

Bandura, A. (2001). Social cognitive theory: An agentic perspective. *Annual Review of Psychology, 52*, 1–26.

Bandura, A. (2006). Toward a psychology of human agency. *Perspectives on Psychological Science, 1*(2), 164–180.

Barron, B., & Darling-Hammond, L. (2008). How can we teach for meaningful learning. *Powerful Learning: What We Know About Teaching for Understanding, 1*, 11–16.

Barton, A. C., & Tan, E. (2010). We be burnin'! Agency, identity, and science learning. *The Journal of the Learning Sciences, 19*(2), 187–229.

Barton, A. C., Tan, E., & Rivet, A. (2008). Creating hybrid spaces for engaging school science among urban middle school girls. *American Educational Research Journal, 45*(1), 68–103.

Basu, S., Calabrese Barton, A., Clairmont, N., & Locke, D. (2009). Developing a framework for critical science agency through case study in a conceptual physics context. *Cultural Studies of Science Education, 4*(2), 345–371.

Bates, C. C., & Morgan, D. N. (2018). Literacy leadership: The importance of soft skills. *Literacy Coaching and Professional Development, 72*(3), 412–415.

Berliner, D. (2011). Rational responses to high stakes testing: The case of curriculum narrowing and the harm that follows. *Cambridge Journal of Education, 41*(3), 287–302.

Beucher, R., Handsfield, L., & Hunt, C. (2019). What matter matters? Retaining the critical in new materialist literacy research. *Journal of Literacy Research, 51*(4), 444–479.

Biesta, G., Priestley, M., & Robinson, S. (2015). The role of beliefs in teacher agency. *Teachers and Teaching, 21*(6), 624–640.

Bilac, S. (2012). Supporting students: The foundation of guidance in the classroom. *Schools, 9*(2), 134–146.

Bloome, D., Carter, S. P., Christian, B. M., Otto, S., & Shuart-Faris, N. (2004). *Discourse analysis and the study of classroom language and literacy events: A microethnographic perspective.* Routledge.

Botzakis, S., Burns, L. D., & Hall, L. A. (2014). Literacy reform and Common Core state standards: Recycling the autonomous model. *Language Arts, 91*(4), 223–235.

Boyd, M. P., Edmiston, B., Vasquez, C., & Staples, J. (2020). Song of the week: Developing we-for-us dialogic values. *Australian Journal of Language and Literacy, The, 43*(1), 95.

Brasof, M., & Spector, A. (2016). Teach students about civics through school-wide governance. *Phi Delta Kappan, 97*(7), 63–68.

Brenner, D., & Hiebert, E. H. (2010). If I follow the teachers' editions, isn't that enough? Analyzing reading volume in six core reading programs. *The Elementary School Journal, 110*(3), 347–363.

Bronk, K. C. (2011). The role of purpose in life in healthy identity formation: A grounded model. *New directions for youth development, 2011*(132), 31–44.

Bronk, K. C. (2013). *Purpose in life: A component of optimal youth development.* Springer.

Brown, R. (2009). Teaching for social justice: Exploring the development of student agency through participation in the literacy practices of a mathematics classroom. *Journal of Mathematics Teacher Education, 12*(3), 171–185.

Brown, R. (2020). Re-conceptualizing the development of agency in the school mathematics classroom. *Theory Into Practice, 59*(2), 139–149.

Cammarota, J., & Romero, A. (2011). Participatory action research for high school students: Transforming policy, practice, and the personal with social justice education. *Educational Policy, 25*(3), 488–506.

Campano, G. (2007). *Immigrant students and literacy: Reading, writing, and remembering.* Teachers College Press.

Campano, G., Ghiso, M. P., Badaki, O., & Kannan, C. (2020). Agency as collectivity: Community-based research for educational equity. *Theory Into Practice, 59*(2), 223–233.

Campano, G., Ghiso, M. P., & Sanchez, L. (2013). "Nobody knows the . . . amount of a person": Elementary students critiquing dehumanization through organic critical literacies. *Research in the Teaching of English, 48*(1), 98–125.

Cavagnetto, A. R., Hand, B., & Premo, J. (2020). Supporting student agency in science. *Theory Into Practice, 59*(2), 128–138.

Certo, J., Moxley, K., Reffitt, K., & Miller, J. A. (2010). I learned how to talk about a book: Children's perceptions of literature circles across grade and ability levels. *Literacy Research and Instruction, 49*(3), 243–263.

Christian, B., & Bloome, D. (2004). Learning to read is who you are. *Reading & Writing Quarterly, 20*(4), 365–384.

Clarke, S. N., Howley, I., Resnick, L., & Rosé, C. P. (2016). Student agency to participate in dialogic science discussions. *Learning, Culture and Social Interaction, 10*, 27–39.

Cochran-Smith, M. (2005). The new teacher education: For better or for worse? *Educational Researcher, 34*(7), 3–17.

Cochran-Smith, M. (2020). Accountability and initial teacher education reform: A perspective from abroad. *Wales Journal of Education, 22*(1), 61–83.

Cochran-Smith, M., & Lytle, S. L. (2009). *Inquiry as stance: Practitioner research for the next generation.* Teachers College Press.

Cook-Sather, A. (2020). Student voice across contexts: Fostering student agency in today's schools. *Theory Into Practice, 59*(2), 182–191.

Cooren, F. (2010). *Action and agency in dialogue: Passion, incarnation and ventriloquism* (Vol. 6). John Benjamins.

Cowie, B., & Khoo, E. (2017). Accountability through access, authenticity and advocacy when researching with young children. *International Journal of Inclusive Education, 21*(3), 234–247.

Cramer, E., Little, M. E., & McHatton, P. A. (2018). Equity, equality, and standardization: Expanding the conversations. *Education and Urban Society, 50*, 483–501.

Czerniewicz, L., Williams, K., & Brown, C. (2009). Students make a plan: Understanding student agency in constraining conditions. *ALT-J Research in Learning Technology, 17*(2), 75–88.

Damon, W. (2008). *The path to purpose: Helping our children find their calling in life.* Simon & Schuster.

Damon, W., Menon, J., & Bronk, K. C. (2003). The development of purpose during adolescence. *Applied Developmental Science, 7*(3), 119–128.

Daniels, H. (2002). *Literature circles: Voice and choice in book clubs and reading groups*. Stenhouse.

Deci, E. L., & Ryan, R. M. (1985). Conceptualizations of intrinsic motivation and self-determination. In E. Aronson (Ed.), *Intrinsic motivation and self-determination in human behavior* (pp. 11–40). Springer.

Deci, E. L., & Ryan, R. M. (2000). The "what" and "why" of goal pursuits: Human needs and the self-determination of behavior. *Psychological Inquiry, 11,* 227–268.

Delpit, L. (2001). Other people's children. *Harvard Educational Review, 56*(4), 379–385.

de Marrais, K. B., & LeCompte, M. (1995). *The way schools work* (2nd ed.). Allyn & Bacon.

Donnor, J. K., & Shockley, K. G. (2010). Leaving us behind: A political economic interpretation of NCLB and the miseducation of African American males. *Educational Foundations, 24,* 43–54.

Doyle, W. (1983). Academic work. *Review of Educational Research, 53*(2), 159–199.

Duckworth, A. L. (2017). *Grit—Why passion and resilience are the secrets to success*. Vermilion.

Duffy, G. G. (2002). Visioning and the development of outstanding teachers. *Reading Research & Instruction, 41*(4), 331–343.

Dweck, C. S. (2012). *Mindset: How you can fulfill your potential*. Constable & Robinson.

Dyson, A. H. (1984). Learning to write/Learning to do school: Emergent writers' interpretations of school literacy tasks. *Research in the Teaching of English, 18*(3), 233–264.

Dyson, A. H. (1986). Transitions and tensions: Interrelationships between the drawing, talking, and dictating of young children. *Research in the Teaching of English, 20*(4), 379–409.

Dyson, A. H. (1997). *Writing superheroes: Contemporary childhood, popular culture, and classroom literacy*. Teachers College Press.

Dyson, A. H. (2003). *The brothers and sisters learn to write: Popular literacies in childhood and school culture*. Teachers College Press.

Dyson, A. H. (2020). "This isn't my real writing": The fate of children's agency in too-tight curricula. *Theory Into Practice, 59*(2), 119–127.

Edwards, A., & D'Arcy, C. (2004). Relational agency and disposition in sociocultural accounts of learning to teach. *Educational Review, 56*(2), 147–155.

Edwards, A., & Mackenzie, L. (2005). Steps towards participation: The social support of learning trajectories. *International Journal of Lifelong Education, 24*(4), 287–302.

Evans, P., & Liu, M. Y. (2019). Psychological needs and motivational outcomes in a high school orchestra program. *Journal of Research in Music Education, 67*(1), 83–105.

Ferguson, D. L., Hanreddy, A., & Draxton, S. (2011). Giving students voice as a strategy for improving teacher practice. *London Review of Education, 9*(1), 55–70.

Ferguson, R. F., Phillips, S. F., Rowley, J. F., & Friedlander, J. W. (2015). *The influence of teaching beyond standardized test scores: Engagement, mindsets, and agency.* Achievement Gap Initiative, Harvard University. http://www.agi.harvard.edu/publications.php

Ferrada, J. S., Bucholtz, M., & Corella, M. (2020). "Respeta mi idioma": Latinx Youth Enacting Affective Agency. *Journal of Language, Identity & Education, 19*(2), 79–94.

Fisher, D., & Frey, N. (2018). Raise reading volume through access, choice, discussion, and book talks. *The Reading Teacher, 72*(1), 89–97.

Flores, N. (2016). Combatting marginalized spaces in education through language architecture. *Penn GSE Perspectives on Urban Education, 13*(1), 1–3.

Flores, N., & Rosa, J. (2015). Undoing appropriateness: Raciolinguistic ideologies and language diversity in education. *Harvard Educational Review, 85*(2), 149–171.

Freire, P. (1970). Cultural action and conscientization. *Harvard Educational Review, 40*(3), 452–477.

Freire, P. (2005). Pedagogy of the oppressed. *Continuum.*

Gambrell, L. B., Malloy, J. A., & Mazzoni, S. A. (2011). Evidence-based best practices in comprehensive literacy instruction. In L. M. Morrow & L. B. Gambrell (Eds.), *Best practices in literacy instruction* (4th ed.) (pp. 11–36). Guilford.

Garcia, A., Mirra, N., Morrell, E., Martinez, A., & Scorza, D. A. (2015). The council of youth research: Critical literacy and civic agency in the digital age. *Reading & Writing Quarterly, 31*(2), 151–167.

Garud, R., Hardy, C., & Maguire, S. (2007). Institutional entrepreneurship as embedded agency: An introduction to the special issue. *Organization Studies, 28*(7), 957–969.

Gay, G. (2002). Preparing for culturally responsive teaching. *Journal of Teacher Education, 53*(2), 106–116.

Genishi, C., & Dyson, A. H. (2015). *Children, language, and literacy: Diverse learners in diverse times.* Teachers College Press.

Ghiso, M. P. (2011). Writing that matters: Collaborative inquiry and authoring practices in a first-grade class. *Language Arts, 88*(5), 346–355.

Giddens, A. (1979). *Central problems in social theory: Action, structure, and contradiction in social analysis.* University of California Press.

Ginns, I., Heirdsfield, A., Atweh, B., & Watters, J. J. (2001). Beginning teachers becoming professionals through action research. *Educational Action Research, 9*(1), 111–133.

Giroux, H., & Simon, R. (1989). Popular culture and critical pedagogy: Every-day life as a basis for curriculum knowledge. In H. A. Giroux & P. McLaren (Eds.), *Critical pedagogy, the state and cultural struggle* (pp. 236–252). State University of New York Press.

Green, T. L. (2017). Community-based equity audits: A practical approach for educational leaders to support equitable community-school improvements. *Educational Administration Quarterly, 53*(1), 3–39.

Greene, M. (1988). *The dialectic of freedom.* Teachers College Press.

Gultom, F., Gultom, F., Kosasih, M., Li, M., Lie, J., Lorenzo, C., & Setiawan, D. (2019). What is home? A collaborative multimodal inquiry project by transnational youth in South Philadelphia. *in:cite journal, 2,* 4–24.

Gutstein, E. (2007). "And that's just how it starts": Teaching mathematics and developing student agency. *Teachers College Record, 109*(2), 420–448.

Hammerness, K. (2001). Teachers' visions: The role of personal ideals in school reform. *Journal of Educational Change, 2,* 143–163.

Hargreaves, A. (2019). Teacher collaboration: 30 years of research on its nature, forms, limitations and effects. *Teachers and Teaching, 25*(5), 603–621.

Hatt, B. (2007). Street smarts vs. book smarts: The figured world of smartness in the lives of marginalized, urban youth. *The Urban Review, 39*(2), 145–166.

Hatt, B. (2012). Smartness as a cultural practice in schools. *American Educational Research Journal, 49*(3), 438–460.

Hatt, B., & Urrieta, L. (2020). Contesting the Alamo and smartness: Theorizing student identities, agency, and learning within the contentious practices of US classrooms. *Theory Into Practice, 59*(2), 202–212.

Hill, P. L., Burrow, A. L., & Bronk, K. C. (2016). Persevering with positivity and purpose: An examination of purpose commitment and positive affect as predictors of grit. *Journal of Happiness Studies, 17*(1), 257–269.

Hilppö, J., Lipponen, L., Kumpulainen, K., & Virlander, M. (2016). Sense of agency and everyday life: Children's perspective. *Learning, Culture and Social Interaction, 10,* 50–59.

Hoffman, J. V., & Duffy, G. G. (2016). Does thoughtfully adaptive teaching actually exist? A challenge to teacher educators. *Theory Into Practice, 55*(3), 172–179.

Holland, D., & Lave, J. (2009). Social practice theory and the historical production of persons. *Action: An International Journal of Human Activity Theory, 2,* 1–15.

Holland, D. C., Lachicotte, W., Skinner, D., & Cain, C. (2001). *Identity and agency in cultural worlds.* Harvard University Press.

hooks, b. (1990). Homeplace (a site of resistance). In b. hooks, *Yearning: Race, gender, and cultural politics* (pp. 383–390). South End Press.

Howard, C. M., & Miller, S. (2018). Pay-for-performance reform programs: It's more than the money! *Urban Education.* https://doi.org/0.1177/0042085918801436

Inden, R. (1990). *Imagining India*. Wiley.

Ivey, G., & Johnston, P. H. (2013). Engagement with young adult literature: Outcomes and processes. *Reading Research Quarterly, 48*(3), 255–275.

Jackson, D. B. (2003). Education reform as if student agency mattered: Academic microculture and student identity. *Phi Delta Kappan, 84*(8), 579–585.

Jackson, P. N. (1968). *Life in classrooms*. Holt, Rinehart and Winston.

Jiang, S., Shen, J., Smith, B. E., & Kibler, K. W. (2020). Science identity development: How multimodal composition mediates student role-taking as scientist in a media-rich learning environment. *Educational Technology Research and Development, 68*, 3187–3182.

Johnson, C. (2017). Learning basic programming concepts with game maker. *International Journal of Computer Science Education in Schools, 1*(2), 1–20.

Johnson, J. (2019). Using found poetry to cultivate student literacy, empathy, and creativity. *Social Studies Research and Practice, 14*(3), 335–348.

Johnston, P. H. (2004). *Choice words: How our language affects children's learning.* Stenhouse.

Johnston, P., Dozier, C., & Smit, J. (2016). How language supports adaptive teaching through a responsive learning culture. *Theory Into Practice, 55*(3), 189–196.

Keiler, L. S. (2018). Teachers' roles and identities in student-centered classrooms. *International Journal of STEM Education, 5*(1), 34.

Kohli, R., Pizarro, M., & Nevárez, A. (2017). The "new racism" of K–12 schools: Centering critical research on racism. *Review of Research in Education, 41*(1), 182–202.

Koshy, S. I., & Mariano, J. M. (2011). Promoting youth purpose: A review of the literature. *New Directions for Youth Development, 2011*(132), 13–29.

Kuby, C., & Vaughn, M. (2015). Young children's identities becoming: Exploring agency in the creation of multimodal literacies. *Journal of Early Childhood Literacy, 15*(1), 1–40.

Lewis, C., Enciso, P. E., & Moje, E. B. (Eds.). (2007). *Reframing sociocultural research on literacy: Identity, agency, and power*. Erlbaum.

Lortie, D. (1975). *Schoolteacher: A sociological study*. University of Chicago Press.

Madda, C. L., Griffo, V. B., Pearson, P. D., & Raphael, T. E. (2011). Balance in comprehensive literacy instruction: Evolving conceptions. In L. M. Morrow & L. B. Gambrell (Eds.), *Best practices in literacy instruction* (4th ed.) (pp. 37–63). Guilford.

Mariano, J. M., Going, J., Schrock, K., & Sweeting, K. (2011). Youth purpose and the perception of social supports among African-American girls. *Journal of Youth Studies, 14*(8), 921–937.

Marinak, B. A., & Gambrell, L. B. (2016). *No more reading for junk: Best practices for motivating readers*. Heinemann.

Mariscal, K., Velásquez, Y., Agüero, A., & Urrieta, L. (2017). Latina urban education: At the crossroads of intersectional violence. In W. T. Pink &

G. W. Noblit (Eds.), *International handbook of urban education* (2nd ed., pp. 875–886). Springer.

Massey, D. D., & Wall, A. (2020). Cultivating teacher candidates who support student agency: Four promising practices. *Theory Into Practice, 59*(2), 172–181.

Mayes, E., Bakhshi, S., Wasner, V., Mohammad, M., Bishop, D. C., Groundwater-Smith, S., Prior, M., Nelson, E., McGregor, J., Carson, K., Webb, R., Flashman, L., McLaughlin, C., & Cowley, E. (2017). What can a conception of power do? Theories and images of power in student voice work. *International Journal of Student Voice, 2*(1), 1–44.

McLaren, P. (2008). Critical pedagogy: A look at the major concepts. In A. Darder, M. P. Baltodano, & R. D. Torres (Eds.), *The critical pedagogy reader* (pp. 61–81). Routledge.

Mehta, J. (2015, April 17). The problem with grit. *Education Week.* https://blogs.edweek.org/edweek/learning_deeply/2015/04/the_problem_with_grit.html

Mendoza, E., Kirshner, B., & Gutiérrez, K. D. (Eds.). (2018). *Power, equity and (re)design: Bridging learning and critical theories in learning ecologies for youth.* IAP.

Merga, M. K., & Mat Roni, S. (2018). Children's perceptions of the importance and value of reading. *Australian Journal of Education, 62*(2), 135–153.

Merritt, J., Lee, M. Y., Rillero, P., & Kinach, B. M. (2017). Problem-based learning in K–8 mathematics and science education: A literature review. *Interdisciplinary Journal of Problem-Based Learning, 11*(2). DOI: https://doi.org/10.7771/1541-5015.1674

Mitra, D. (2004). The significance of students: Can increasing "student voice" in schools lead to gains in youth development? *Teachers College Record, 106*(4), 651–688.

Moses, L., Rylak, D., Reader, T., Hertz, C., & Ogden, M. (2020). Educators' perspectives on supporting student agency. *Theory Into Practice, 59*(2), 213–222.

National Governors Association Center for Best Practices & Council of Chief State School Officers. (2010). *Common Core state standards for English language arts and literacy in history/social studies, science, and technical subjects.* Authors.

Nieto, S. (2006). Teaching as political work: Learning from courageous and caring teachers. Paper given during the annual Longfellow Lecture. Sarah Lawrence College. https://www.sarahlawrence.edu/media/cdi/pdf/Occasional%20Papers/CDI_Occasional_Paper_2006_Nieto.pdf

No Child Left Behind Act of 2001, Public Law No.107-110, 20 U.S.C. § 6319 (2002).

Oakeshott, M., & Fuller, T. (1989). *The voice of liberal learning: Michael Oakeshott on education.* Yale University Press.

Onosko, J. (2011). Race to the Top leaves children and future citizens behind: The devastating effects of centralization, standardization, and high stakes accountability. *Democracy and Education, 19*(2). https://democracyeducationjournal.org/home/vol19/iss2/1

Pearson, P. D., & Gallagher, M. C. (1983). The instruction of reading comprehension. *Contemporary Educational Psychology, 8*(3), 317–344.

Pearson, P. D., Raphael, T. E., Benson, V. L., & Madda, C. L. (2007). Balance in comprehensive literacy instruction: Then and now. In L. B. Gambrell, L. M. Morrow, & M. Pressley (Eds.), *Best practices in literacy instruction* (2nd ed., pp. 30–54). Guilford.

Pintrich, P., & García, T. (1993). Intraindividual differences in students' motivation and self-regulated learning. *German Journal of Educational Psychology, 7*(3), 99–107.

Pintrich, P. R., & Garcia, T. (2012). Self-regulated learning in college students: Knowledge, strategies, and motivation. In P. R. Pintrich, D. Brown, & C. E. Weinstein (Eds), *Student motivation, cognition, and learning* (pp. 129–150). Routledge.

Pizzolato, J. E., Brown, E. L., & Kanny, M. A. (2012). Purpose plus: Supporting youth purpose, control, and academic achievement. *New Directions for Student Leadership, 132*, 75–88.

Pressley, M., Allington, R. L., Wharton-McDonald, R., Block, C. C., & Morrow, L. M. (2001). *Learning to read: Lessons from exemplary first-grade classrooms.* Guilford.

Purcell-Gates, V., Duke, N. K., & Martineau, J. A. (2007). Learning to read and write: Roles of authentic experience and explicit teaching. *Reading Research Quarterly, 42*(1), 8–45.

Quinn, S., & Owen, S. (2016). Digging deeper: Understanding the power of "student voice." *Australian Journal of Education, 60*(1), 60–72.

Raphael, T. E., Florio-Ruane, S., & George, M. (2001). Book club "plus": A conceptual framework to organize literacy instruction. *Language Arts, 79*(2), 159–168.

Ravitch, D. (Ed.). (2010). *Debating the future of American education: Do we meet national standards and assessments?* Brookings Institution.

Reeve, J., & Shin, S. H. (2020). How teachers can support students' agentic engagement. *Theory Into Practice, 59*(2), 150–161.

Reyes, R., III. (2009). "Key interactions" as agency and empowerment: Providing a sense of the possible to marginalized, Mexican-descent students. *Journal of Latinos and Education, 8*(2), 105–118.

Robertson, D. A., Padesky, L. B., & Brock, C. H. (2020). Cultivating student agency through teachers' professional learning. *Theory Into Practice, 59*(2), 192–201.

Rogoff, B., Callanan, M., Gutiérrez, K. D., & Erickson, F. (2016). The organization of informal learning. *Review of Research in Education, 40*(1), 356–401.

Ryan, R. M., & Deci, E. L. (2000). Self-determination theory and the facilitation of intrinsic motivation, social development, and well-being. *American Psychologist, 55*(1), 68–78.

Ryan, R. M., & Deci, E. L. (2017). *Self-determination theory: Basic psychological needs in motivation, development, and wellness.* Guilford.

Sawyer, R. K. (2004). Creative teaching: Collaborative discussion as disciplined improvisation. *Educational Researcher, 33*(2), 12–20.

Scherff, L. (2005). *Thirteen years of schooling: What students really think.* Scarecrow Education.

Schipper, T. M., van der Lans, R. M., de Vries, S., Goei, S. L., & van Veen, K. (2020). Becoming a more adaptive teacher through collaborating in lesson study? Examining the influence of lesson study on teachers' adaptive teaching practices in mainstream secondary education. *Teaching and Teacher Education, 88*, 102961.

Sergiovanni, T. J. (2001). *Leadership: What's in it for schools?* Routledge.

Sharma, A. (2008). Making (electrical) connections: Exploring student agency in a school in India. *Science Education, 92*(2), 297–319.

Shulman, L. S., & Shulman, J. (2004). How and what teachers learn: A shifting perspective. *Journal of Curriculum Studies, 36*, 257–271.

Snyder, C. R., Harris, C., Anderson, J. R., Holleran, S. A., Irving, L. M., Sigmon, S. T., & Harney, P. (1991). The will and the ways: Development and validation of an individual-differences measure of hope. *Journal of personality and social psychology, 60*(4), 570–585.

Souto-Manning, M. (2010). *Freire, teaching, and learning: Culture circles across contexts* (Vol. 350). Peter Lang.

Summers, J. J., & Falco, L. D. (2020). The development and validation of a new measure of adolescent purpose. *The Journal of Experimental Education, 88*(1), 47–71.

Tal, T., Krajcik, J. S., & Blumenfeld, P. C. (2006). Urban schools' teachers enacting project based science. *Journal of Research in Science Teaching, 43*(7), 722–745.

Tobin, K., & Llena, R. (2010). Producing and maintaining culturally adaptive teaching and learning of science in urban schools. In C. Murphy & K. Scantlebury (Eds.), *Coteaching in international context: Cultural studies of science education* (pp. 79–103). Springer.

Toshalis, E. (2015). *Make me! Understanding and engaging student resistance in school.* Harvard Education Press.

Tran, L. T., & Vu, T. T. P. (2018). "Agency in mobility": Towards a conceptualisation of international student agency in transnational mobility. *Educational Review, 70*(2), 167–187.

Turner, J. C. (1995). The influence of classroom contexts on young children's motivation for literacy. *Reading Research Quarterly, 30*(3), 410–441.

Tyack, D., & Cuban, L. (1997). *Tinkering toward utopia: A century of public school reform.* Harvard University Press.

U.S. Department of Education. (2009, November). *Race to the Top program executive summary*. https://www2.ed.gov/programs/racetothetop/index.html

U.S. Department of Education. (2015). *Every Student Succeeds Act (ESSA)*. https://www.ed.gov/ESSA

van Lier, L. (2008). Agency in the classroom. In J. P. Lantolf & M. E. Poehner (Eds.), *Sociocultural theory and teaching of second languages* (pp. 1–14). Equinox.

Vaughn, M. (2013). Examining teacher agency: Why did Les leave the building? *New Educator, 9*(2), 119–134.

Vaughn, M. (2014). The role of student agency: Exploring openings during literacy instruction. *Teaching and Learning: The Journal of Natural Inquiry & Reflective Practice, 28*(1), 4–16.

Vaughn, M. (2016). Re-envisioning literacy in a teacher inquiry group in a Native American context. *Literacy Research and Instruction, 55*(1), 24–47.

Vaughn, M. (2018). Making sense of student agency in the early grades. *Phi Delta Kappan, 99*(7), 62–66.

Vaughn, M. (2019). Adaptive teaching during reading instruction: A multi-case study. *Reading Psychology, 41*(1), 1–33.

Vaughn, M. (2020). What is student agency and why is it needed now more than ever? Student agency: Theoretical implications for practice. *Theory Into Practice, 59*(2), 109–118.

Vaughn, M., & Faircloth, B. (2013). Teaching with a purpose in mind: Cultivating a vision for teaching. *The Professional Educator, 37*(2), 1–12.

Vaughn, M., & Kuby, C. R. (2019). Fostering critical, relational visionaries: Autoethnographic processes in teacher education. *Action in Teacher Education, 41*(2), 117–136.

Vaughn, M., & Parsons, S. A. (2013). Teachers as innovators: Instructional adaptations opening spaces for enhanced literacy learning. *Language Arts Journal, 91*(2), 303–309.

Vaughn, M., Premo, J., Erickson, D., & McManus, C. (2020). Student agency in literacy: Validation of the Student Agency Profile (StAP). *Reading Psychology, 42*(1), 533–558.

Vaughn, M., Premo, J. T., Sotirovska, V., & Erickson, D. (2019). Evaluating agency in literacy using the Student Agency Profile (StAP). *The Reading Teacher, 73*(4), 427–441.

Vaughn, M., Scales, R. Q., Stevens, E., Kline, S., Barrett-Tatum, J., Van Wig, A., Yoder, K. K., & Wellman, D. (2019). Understanding literacy adoption policies across contexts: A multi-state examination of literacy curriculum decision-making. *Journal of Curriculum Studies*. https://doi.org/10.1080/00220272.2019.1683233

Veiga, F., Garcia, F., Reeve, J., Wentzel, K., & Garcia, O. (2015). When adolescents with high self-concept lose their engagement in school. *Revista de Psicodidáctica, 2*, 305–320.

Vygotsky, L. S. (1978). *Mind in society: The development of higher psychological processes.* Harvard University Press.

Wan, G., & Gut, D. M. (Eds.). (2011). *Bringing schools into the 21st century* (Vol. 13). Springer.

Webb, S., Massey, D., Goggans, M., & Flajole, K. (2019). Thirty-five years of the gradual release of responsibility: Scaffolding toward complex and responsive teaching. *The Reading Teacher, 73*(1), 75–83.

Wehmeyer, M. L., Kelchner, K., & Richards. S. (1996). Essential characteristics of self-determined behaviors of adults with mental retardation and developmental disabilities. *American Journal on Mental Retardation, 100,* 632–642.

Wenger, E. (1998). *Communities of practice: Learning, meaning, and identity.* Cambridge University Press.

Wigfield, A., & Cambria, J. (2010). Students' achievement values, goal orientations, and interest: Definitions, development, and relations to achievement outcomes. *Developmental Review, 30*(1), 1–35.

Wigfield, A., & Eccles, J. S. (2000). Expectancy-value theory of achievement motivation. *Contemporary Educational Psychology, 25,* 68–81.

Winne, P. H., & Marx, R. W. (1982). Students' and teachers' views of thinking processes for classroom learning. *The Elementary School Journal, 82*(5), 493–518.

Wortham, S. (2006). *Learning identity: The joint emergence of social identification and academic learning.* Cambridge University Press.

Yen, C. J., Konold, T. R., & McDermott, P. A. (2004). Does learning behavior augment cognitive ability as an indicator of academic achievement? *Journal of School Psychology, 42*(2), 157–169.

York, A., & Kirshner, B. (2015). How positioning shapes opportunities for student agency in schools. *Teachers College Record, 117*(13), 103–118.

Zaccor, K. M. (2018). Connecting with students through a critical, participatory curriculum: An exploration into a high school history teacher's construction of teacher–student relationships. *Urban Education.* https://doi.org/10.1177/0042085918794779

Zhang, H., Estabrooks, L., & Perry, A. (2019). Bringing invention education into middle school science classrooms: A case study. *Technology & Innovation, 20*(3), 235–250.

Index

About the Author

Margaret Vaughn is an associate professor at Washington State University. She has written several research articles that address the ways in which instructional contexts are able to support student agency and various aspects of literacy learning and teacher practice. She has received several professional awards, including the Literacy Research Association Research Paper Award, (2020), American Educational Research Association (AERA) Review of Research Award (2019), AERA Classroom Observation Exemplary Paper Award (2018), Association of Teacher Educators (ATE) Distinguished Research in Teacher Education Award (2017), the Haslett Distinguished Faculty Fellow award (2013–2014), and the Horace Mann National Teacher Education Award (2007). She is heavily invested in supporting elementary schools and continues to engage in professional development with teachers to support meaningful literacy opportunities for all students centered on supporting students' cultural backgrounds and linguistic strengths.